THE ART OF HEALTHY EATING
grain free low carb reinvented
SLOW COOKER

The Art of Healthy Eating: Slow Cooker

Copyright © 2013 by Maria Emmerich

All rights reserved. No part of this book may be reproduced or transmitted in any form or by any means without written permission of the author.

ISBN 978-0-9885124-5-0

Published by Maria and Craig Emmerich, printed by Thomson Shore.

THE ART OF HEALTHY EATING
grain free low carb reinvented
SLOW COOKER

Maria Emmerich

Thank You

I want to dedicate this book to you, yes you. It is because of you and your support that has made this all possible. About 4 months after we adopted our baby boys, my husband, Craig, lost his job. We kept this secret for awhile... it was such a scary time for us and Craig didn't want to feel like he was failing his family. But thanks to all of you, my boys have the best stay-at-home dad EVER! It is because of all of your support with purchasing my books and pantry items from my astore that helps keep us going.

I once heard someone say, "If you want to hear God laugh, tell him what you have planned!" That statement couldn't have been more true for the past few years of my life. I was totally a planner, and the more I tried to control how things happened, the more frustrated I got. All of the trials I have gone through helped push me in the right direction to my nutrition business.

Thank you... thank you .... thank you.... from Maria, Craig, Micah and Kai!

Thank you Jamie for the covers of all of my books! Thank you Rebecca for all your help and friendship. Thank you Mavis and Janet for helping with editing. Also, thanks to Jera Publishing for the layout and Thomson Shore for the printing.

Contents

MAIN DISHES: AMERICAN

MAIN DISHES: ITALIAN

Introduction

It is Monday morning and the whole family is running late. The bus is about to pick up the kids and they haven't eaten anything yet. So you pour them a glass of no-sugar added "all natural" grape juice and toss a Pop-Tart their way. But they made it onto the bus and no one was late, WHEW! Thank goodness for pre-packaged "food."

No time for breakfast meant no time to pack their lunch either, so your children ate school lunch that day; chicken nuggets, mashed potatoes, a bun, fruit cocktail and chocolate milk. After school programs and sports keep your kids at school until 4:30, so they grab a granola bar and Gatorade from their backpack to keep their energy up. Once all of the activities are over, mom is tired from driving all over the place, picking up the kids so she throws in frozen pizza with a side of garlic bread with some skim milk. Then a bowl of Lucky Charms for a bed-time snack (they are made with "Whole Grains" now). Does that sound like you?

Tuesday was a better day. Everyone had time for breakfast so the kids had Honey Nut Cheerios, Skim milk and a banana sliced on top. You packed a lunch of Lunch-ables, Goldfish crackers and a juice box. The after-school snack was yogurt covered raisins and Gatorade. You had time to make dinner so you made spaghetti with a side of garlic bread, salad with fat-free French dressing and skim milk for dinner…oh, and fat-free frozen yogurt for dessert! You think you

did better today…but did you? This equals about 100 teaspoons or over 2 cups of sugar in your bloodstream. Do you know what a normal blood sugar level is? 1 cup? 2 cups? NO, 1 TEASPOON of sugar is a normal blood sugar! For adults, children, teens and babies. Blood sugar increases insulin and insulin is TOXIC to our bodies and cells.

Dr. Stephen Sondike, Program Director for NEW (Nutrition, Exercise and Weight Management) Kids Program at Children's Hospital of Wisconsin, disagrees with the assertion that low-carb diets make kids sluggish. He says the opposite is true. "Kids get tired when they eat a breakfast high in carbohydrates and their blood sugar drops at around 10:00 am." Sondike says that a breakfast consisting of a bagel and a glass of orange juice—both high-carb items—causes a temporary spike in blood sugar for a high-energy early morning, but results in a mid-morning "crash" that leaves bodies listless and craving sugar. "When you eat more sugar, your body makes less sugar, so you need more sugar," Sondike explains. "The candy and coke makers love it when people eat high-carb breakfasts because they need that fix around 10:00 am when their sugar drops."

Insulin and its counterbalancing hormone, glucagon, are in charge of controlling metabolism. The word insulin may immediately call up an association with diabetes, and this is totally valid. Controlling blood sugar is insulin's most important job. Many people with heart disease, high cholesterol, diabetes, high blood pressure in their families have inherited a tendency for their insulin sensors on the cells to malfunction from years of high sugar and starch consumption. As these sensors become tired, insulin resistance develops. Since it's essential to get the sugar out of the blood and into the cells, the pancreas overcompensates by making more and more insulin to force the tired sensors to work. This starts a detrimental cycle of needing ever more insulin to keep the process going. Some people become so resistant to insulin that the amount necessary to make the sensors respond and clear the sugar from the blood is more than their pancreas can make; that is when that person becomes diabetic.

Excess insulin causes a variety of other detrimental problems; it increases the production of cholesterol in the liver; thickens the walls of the arteries, causing high blood pressure; the kidneys retain salt and fluid; and it tells our fat cells to store excess starch and sugar.

Insulin's actions are countered by glucagon. Glucagon alerts the liver to slow down triglyceride and cholesterol production, the kidneys to release excess salt and fluid, the artery wall to relax and lower blood pressure, and the fat cells to release stored fat to be burned for energy. But, insulin is stronger than glucagon so when it is high, it suppress glucagon's actions. After a childhood of sugar and starch consumption, metabolic syndrome and insulin resistance happens. This is why what we feed our children is so important.

What we eat controls the production of these hormones. This book will teach you how to stimulate glucagon by keeping insulin low, which will allow the metabolism to heal and the malfunctioning sensors to regain sensitivity. Once this healing occurs, the metabolic disturbances that elevated insulin will improve or disappear; cholesterol and triglycerides return to normal, blood pressure returns to normal, blood sugar stabilizes and you can achieve a normal body weight. There's no need to spend huge amounts of money on

medications to put a "band-aid" over these problems. I have seen it time and time again; nutrition is key to a healthy body. You can pay the doctor or you can pay the farmer.

You wouldn't put diesel in a gasoline engine and expect it to run…but that is what American's are guilty of doing to their bodies on a daily basis. We consistently fuel our bodies with processed, pre-packaged foods that evolutionary science has proven to make our bodies stop running efficiently; I was guilty of this also.

I grew up with a passion for sports as well as food; my body shape revealed my two loves. I was athletic yet fat. Weight loss was difficult until I found the right foods and ditched the fake foods, then it became easy. Fat and frustrated, I finally decided to throw out the government recommendations of more "whole grains." I included more protein; especially for breakfast…skim milk in your Cheerio's doesn't count as a protein! After decades of being told by marketing geniuses that "fat free" was the way to lose weight, eating real fat was scary for me. Once I started adding fat to my diet, I slept deeper, felt calmer and better in that first week than I ever had.

I learned the secrets of the hormone insulin and the lesser known hormone leptin; that by evolving toward a very low-glycemic, high-fat (not just high-protein) diet, I had re-sensitized my biochemistry to these essential hormones which turn off severe food cravings. Best of all, my diet makeover required a lot less self-deprivation than what I suffered when I wasn't losing weight. The nutrient-rich, relatively high-fat dietary approach I have developed for myself, with exotic, little-known replacements for typical high-glycemic starchy foods and sugar are what finally gave me total peace with food; something I never imagined possible. The weight came off, even more than my original goal. I am happy to reveal these exotic tasty weight loss foods; such as almond flour for cookies and coconut flour for cakes. After all, we also need to enjoy the sweetness of life.

The love-hate relationship with food typically starts with innocent dieting and calorie counting, followed by out of control binging that causes dangerous extremes, such as skipping meals, obsessive-compulsive exercise, and purging. It is no wonder that food becomes the enemy; which is an unhappy state to be in. I help clients discover the beauty that nutrition can give us a life free from cravings and weight gain if we choose the right items.

Before my revelation of the biochemistry of food and our weight, I was so proud of my "perfect" diet of whole grains, fruits, and fat-free desserts, but I was still puzzled as to why I had uncontrollable cravings around food. By finding the correct supplements to change my biochemical imbalances, I started a high healthy-fat, grain-free, no starch diet; I finally found peace in my body. I didn't feel deprived or compelled to overeat.

The 'secret' is to control leptin and insulin hormones. Any diet that stops blood sugar and insulin spikes also allows the cells to regain sensitivity to the noteworthy anti-aging, weight and hunger-regulating hormone called leptin. The hardest part is to get my clients to not be afraid of fat because it is almost impossible to obtain this effect without significant amounts of fat in the diet. High protein alone doesn't work because excess protein will also turn to sugar. Low fat, high protein diets will fail to keep your blood sugar from spiking, and will not allow your leptin hormone to increase. Ron Rosedale, MD, author of The Rosedale Diet and a pioneering scientist on the hormone leptin, states, "If you don't get enough fat, you will likely eat too much protein, which then turns to sugar."

I am writing this book to everyone who has been frustrated with the way they feel, kids that don't sleep, children with ADHD, athletes, teenagers struggling with acne and parents who just want to start feeding their family real food again. Nutrition is a huge part of how we feel and operate every day. I love feeling energetic and confident and I want you to also. I was miserable when I constantly deprived myself and felt guilty when I ate. I want you to also find peace and enjoyment with real food; which can turn into holistic peace in your everyday life.

Pesto Fish recipe is on page 146

Specific Ingredients:
Milk

The ingredients used in this cookbook are very specific. I have dissected all the macro and micro-nutrients to create recipes to keep our insulin levels low while keeping flavors high. For example, you will never see skim milk in my recipes for a variety of reasons, which you can read more on my chapter "Milk, Does it Really Do a 'Body Good' ?" in Secrets to a Healthy Metabolism.

UNSWEETENED ALMOND MILK.

It is extremely low in sugar and carbohydrates, and it tastes great. It only has 40 calories per cup versus 90 calories for skim milk.

COCONUT MILK.

It is low in sugar and is healthy for SO many reasons. Here are just some of what studies have shown coconut milk can do for our health...

1 FOCUS AND MOOD. Improves insulin secretion and utilization of blood glucose, this in turn balances children's moods and ability to focus. Helps relieve reduce health risks associated with diabetes.

2 INTESTINAL DISORDERS. Helps relieve symptoms associated with gallbladder disease. Relieves symptoms associated with Crohn's disease, ulcerative colitis, and stomach ulcers. Improves digestion and bowel function. Relieves pain and irritation caused by hemorrhoids. Supports tissue healing and repair of the intestines. Improves digestion and absorption of other nutrients including vitamins, minerals, and amino acids. Reduces problems associated with malabsorption syndrome and cystic fibrosis.

3 ATHLETES: PROVIDES KETONES FOR A QUICK SOURCE ENERGY. Boosts energy and endurance, enhancing physical and athletic performance. This also helps relieve symptoms associated with chronic fatigue syndrome.

4 IMMUNE SYSTEM. Kills viruses that cause influenza, herpes, measles, hepatitis C, SARS, AIDS, and other illnesses. It also kills bacteria that cause ulcers, throat infections, urinary tract infections, gum disease and cavities, pneumonia, and gonorrhea, and other diseases.

5 DIAPER RASH/THRUSH. Kills fungi and yeasts that cause thrush, candida, ringworm, athlete's foot, diaper rash (infections).

6 SKIN DISORDERS. Applied topically helps to form a chemical barrier on the skin to ward off infection. Reduces symptoms associated with psoriasis, eczema, and dermatitis. Supports the natural chemical balance of the skin. Softens skin and helps relieve dryness and flaking. Promotes healthy looking hair and complexion. Provides protection from damaging effects of ultraviolet radiation from the sun. Helps control dandruff.

7 STRONG TEETH AND BONES. Improves calcium and magnesium absorption and supports the development of strong bones and teeth which is extremely important during the teenage years.

8 HEART HEALTH. Reduces inflammation. It is heart healthy; improves cholesterol ratio reducing risk of heart disease. Protects arteries from injury that causes atherosclerosis and thus protects against heart disease.

9 AGING. Helps to protect the body from harmful free radicals that promote premature aging and degenerative disease. Does not deplete the body's antioxidant reserves like other oils do. Improves utilization of essential fatty acids and protects them from oxidation. Prevents wrinkles, sagging skin, and age spots.

10 KIDNEY STONES. Helps protect against kidney disease and bladder infections. Dissolves kidney stones.

11 WEIGHT LOSS. It is lower in calories than all other fats and it supports thyroid function. It promotes weight loss by increasing metabolic rate. Is utilized by the body to produce energy in preference to being stored as body fat like other dietary fats. Medium chained triglycerides produce ketones (energy) rather than being stored as fat.

12 RELIEVES STRESS ON PANCREAS AND ENZYME SYSTEMS OF THE BODY. Reduces symptoms associated with pancreatitis.

13 Does not form harmful by-products when heated to normal cooking temperature like other vegetable oils.

HEMP MILK.

Hemp milk is growing in popularity because of its flavor and texture. It also has lots of nutrients including calcium, tons of vitamins, minerals, and essential omega-3 and -6 fatty acids.

Milk Substitutions (Per Cup)					
Item	Rating	Carbs	Sugars	Fiber	Calories
Skim Milk	Bad	13	13	0	91
Unsweetened Hemp Milk	OK	1	0	0	60
Unsweetened Almond Milk	Best	2	0	1	40
Unsweetened Coconut Milk	Best	1	0	0	50

Thai beef and pasta salad recipe is on page 150

Flour

TIP

All flours are not created equal. If you have coconut flour in the house and the recipe calls for almond flour and you use coconut flour instead, your finished product will not turn out. Baking with almond flour also requires using more eggs to provide more structure. Use it in cakes, cookies, and other sweet baked goods. I buy mine here: aff.nuts.com/SF3E

ALMOND FLOUR

In my family we treat corn, carrots, potatoes and rice as starchy foods, as if they were sweets (starch and sugar = excess weight gain). They are all starchy carbohydrates as are the products made from them (chips, cereal, rice cakes and snacks). So we never use alternative flours made from corn, rice or potatoes. 4 grams of carbohydrates from sugar or starch becomes 1 teaspoon of sugar in our body!

Baking with almond flour requires using more eggs to provide more structure. You can use it in cakes, cookies, and other sweet baked goods. I buy mine at aff.nuts.com/SF3E

It is important to use blanched almond flour. Most recipes will not work with unblanched; most almond meal (found at Trader Joe's) is made with unblanched almonds. Unblanched means the dark outside is on the almond; it creates a different texture in baking, which doesn't work as well to create soft baked goods. It makes a fine cookie, but it won't be as soft as a baked item made of 'white flour.' Here are some additional benefits of substituting almond flour for white flour:

1 FOCUS AND MOOD. Almonds contain tryptophan. This amino acid helps with serotonin production (the "feel good" chemical in the brain). When levels of serotonin fall, your body senses starvation. To protect itself, your body starts to crave carbohydrates. Serotonin levels fall after you go too long without eating, and that encourages your body to start filling itself (losing muscle).

2 SLEEP DISORDERS/IMMUNE SYSTEM/ATHLETES (MAGNESIUM). What mineral is needed by every cell in the body, yet odds are you don't get enough of it? Hint: It's not calcium. Give up? It's magnesium. Magnesium deficiencies correlate to Alzheimer's and Parkinson's. Deficiencies also cause muscle spasms, pain, insomnia and fatigue. Magnesium assists in maintaining muscle mass, nerve function, a regular heartbeat, helps our immune system, and keeps bones strong. Diabetics benefit from magnesium as it helps regulate blood sugar levels. In addition, magnesium normalizes blood pressure, and is known to be involved in energy metabolism and protein synthesis. There has been a lot of medical interest in using magnesium to avoid and manage disorders such as cardiovascular disease,

diabetes, and hypertension. Almonds contain more magnesium than oatmeal or even spinach. It is found that magnesium deficiencies increase food cravings.

3 B-VITAMINS. These are our anti-stress vitamins. Vitamin B contents also promote healthy growth of hair as well as nails. I use almond oil on my skin everyday.

4 BONE HEALTH. 1 ounce or about 20-25 almonds has more calcium than ¼ cup of milk! A valuable snack in preventing osteoporosis. You will also build strong bones and teeth with the phosphorus in almonds.

5 CANCER. Almonds are the best whole food source of vitamin E, in the form of alpha-tocopherol, which helps prevent cancer. Using almond flour instead of white flour helps to starve the cancer from high levels of glucose on which it feeds upon.

6 FIBER. The high fiber content helps with weight loss by keeping us full and tapers blood sugar from spiking. The fiber also helps in proper digestion as well as enhancing energy levels.

7 PROTEIN. Almonds have protein. Using almond flour helps give us the protein we need to build proper bones (yes…bones need protein), helps us to focus, builds muscle and staves off sarcopenia. Sarcopenia is a natural process of losing 1% of your muscle per year starting at age 25! Yikes!

COCONUT FLOUR

Coconut flour is unlike any other consisting of 14% coconut oil and 58% dietary fiber! The remaining 28% consists of water, protein, and carbohydrate. It gives baked goods a rich, springy texture but needs a lot more liquid than other flours. For example you only need ½ cup coconut flour for about 6 eggs in a muffin recipe; therefore you end up with a high protein muffin rather than a high carb starch bomb. If you haven't tried coconut flour yet, here are some more excellent reasons to start:

1 LOW CARB AND WEIGHT LOSS. Coconut Flour is ideal for baking. It has fewer digestible carbohydrates than other flours, and it even has fewer than many vegetables! Ideal for keeping blood sugar levels low, which helps weight loss. The high fiber content also promotes a feeling of fullness.

2 GLUTEN FREE. Coconut Flour is gluten-free and hypoallergenic. With as much protein as wheat flour, coconut flour has none of the specific protein in wheat called "gluten". This is an advantage for a growing percentage of the population who have a wheat allergy or sensitivity (many people have it without knowing it).

3 INDIGESTION. Indigestion is caused by excessive hydrochloric acid in the stomach. The acid, which sterilizes food and aids during the digestive process, is secreted by the stomach wall. Usually, the stomach wall is protected by a thick coating of mucus. Persistent high levels of acid cause this coating to break down, and the acid can attack the stomach wall, causing indigestion. Alcohol and acidic foods can further irritate the stomach wall. Coconut Flour consists of the highest percentage of dietary fiber (58%) found in any flour, which improves digestion.

4 CANDIDA, CRAVINGS AND DEPRESSION. The intestines crave good bacteria which improve absorption of vitamins, decrease cravings and increase serotonin. Good bacteria flourish when we eat high-fiber quality food. Yeast causes an imbalance, letting bad bacteria in; they love sugar and starch. Yeast and bad bacteria damage the intestinal wall and produce toxic by-products which can be absorbed into the blood and sent throughout the body. This is how food allergies and leaky-gut syndrome begin.

5 PROTEIN. It is also high in protein which helps increase the Thermic Effect of Food, which increases metabolism. Protein also increases focus and mood.

6 REDUCES GALLSTONES. Gallstones form as a result of a gathering of cholesterol and salts from bile. Bile plays an important role in the absorption of fats from the intestinal tract because it makes fats soluble. Eating high fiber and low carb foods using coconut flour as well as LOTS OF WATER can decrease the chances of gallstones recurring. Galls are released by certain dietary fats.

7 IBS/CROHN'S/COLITUS. Irritable bowel syndrome (IBS) is a malfunction of the nerves in the wall of the bowel that make the bowel muscle contract. It can be connected to stress, vitamin deficiencies and low serotonin levels (depression). One treatment is to consume a high fiber diet; that in combination with coconut oil (a medium chained triglyceride) is VERY helpful for IBS.

8 HEART DISEASE/STROKE/BLOOD PRESSURE. Studies have proven that coconut fiber protects against heart attacks and strokes; it helps reduce cholesterol. Even modest increases in fiber intake can also significantly reduce blood pressure.

9 NO PHYTATES. Most fibrous foods such as seeds, wheats, and oats have phytic acid. This acid causes mineral deficiencies because it binds to minerals in the foods we consume (calcium, zinc and iron). Phytic acid pulls them out of the body resulting in mineral deficiencies. Coconut fiber does not contain phytic acid so it helps improve mineral status when you replace this for wheat flour in your baked goods.

10 HEMORRHOIDS. The high fiber content can help move things along. Just remember to consume extra water when you add in fiber or things can get worse!

11 DIABETICS. Coconut Flour consists of the highest percentage of dietary fiber found in any flour. Fiber helps moderate swings in blood sugar by slowing down the absorption of sugar into the blood stream. This helps keep blood sugar and insulin levels under control.

12 CANCER. Coconut flour is fermentable and produces high amounts of butyric acid which helps in stopping tumor formation. Studies have proven that butyric acid slows the growth of tumor cells and prompts all cells to develop properly. Coconut fiber also promotes good bacteria flourish which boosts our immune system. The high fiber content acts like a broom, sweeping the intestinal contents through the digestive tract. Parasites, toxins, and carcinogens are swept along with the fiber. This prevents toxins that irritate intestinal tissues and cause cancer from getting lodged in the intestinal tract (decreases colon cancer). Since it is low carb, it also helps people maintain a low carb/sugar diet to stop feeding the cancer glucose which the cancer "feeds" upon.

NOTE: Not all coconut flours are created equal. Some brands have different baking properties. I always use Tropical Traditions Coconut Flour.

You can find it here: tropicaltraditions.com

OTHER FLOUR ALTERNATIVES

HAZELNUT FLOUR.

Using this for baked goods gives your dough a sweet nuttiness as well as fiber and iron. After first being diagnosed with a gluten allergy, you may feel tired; this is linked to an iron deficiency. I like to make my muffins with this. Nuts are considered a carbohydrate; however hazelnuts are very low in starch.

FLAXSEED.

This seed has many health benefits such as high-quality protein, fiber, B and C vitamins, iron, and zinc, anti-cancer properties, omega-3 fatty acids, and many other benefits. To use as an egg substitute grind 2 tablespoons flaxseed and add 6 tablespoons boiling water. I have a chocolate flaxseed muffin in the recipe section that is a favorite of many clients.

PSYLLIUM HUSK.

It is a powerful fiber that can be used in place of white flour in many baked goods.

Some benefits include:

1 Maintains healthy cholesterol levels, including a proper balance of HDL and LDL cholesterol.

2 Decreases Constipation: Unlike stimulant laxatives, Psyllium husks are gentle and are not habit forming. Psyllium husks' bulking action makes elimination easier and more comfortable.

3 Reduces Toxins and Estrogen Dominance: Psyllium sweeps waste, excess estrogen and toxins more quickly out of the body, so toxins are not reabsorbed from the colon back into the bloodstream.

4 Reduces the risk of getting colon cancer and hemorrhoids, alleviates bladder and kidney problems, help lower blood glucose in diabetics, helps to make labor easier by dilating the cervix, and helps dieters lose more weight.

5 Natural Antibiotic: It is sold as a cough syrup in many parts of the world. In Argentina it is brewed and strained, then chilled and used to reduce inflammation. In India it is used to treat rheumatism and gout in a mixture of oil and vinegar. Old World remedies used psyllium seeds in a poultice to treat wounds and sores.

6 Gluten-Free: Psyllium husks do not contain any gluten so people who are gluten sensitive can use them.

Flour Substitutions (Per Cup)					
Item	Rating	Carbs	Sugars	Fiber	Calories
Rice Flour (Gluton-Free)	Bad	127	0.2	3.8	578
White Flour	Bad	100	0	4	496
Wheat Flour	Bad	87	0	14	407
Oat Flour	Bad	78	0	12	480
Almond Flour	Best	24	4	12	640
Peanut Flour	Best	21	4	9	196
Coconut Flour	Best	80	0	48	480
Flaxseed Meal	Best	32	0	32	480
Psyllium Husk	Best	80	0	72	280

Sugar Alternatives

If you crave sweets while trying to conquer addictions to food, drugs or alcohol then the sweetness of these alternative sweeteners can help to fulfill these cravings in a healthy manner and not play havoc with weight and blood sugar. Here are the natural sweeteners I use and why.

STEVIA GLYCERITE

Stevia glycerite is a favorite of many people. It is an herb that has been used as a sweetener in South America for hundreds of years. One tip is to look for "stevia glycerite;" which has no bitter aftertaste as compared to plain "stevia. It is widely used all over the world. In Japan, it claims 58% of the sweetener market, and was used in Japanese Diet Coke until the company replaced it with aspartame to "standardize" worldwide.

CALORIES	0
SWEETNESS	300 times sweeter than sugar
CONVERSION	1 tsp stevia = 1 cup of sugar

WHY I USE IT: It is great for cooking, because it maintains flavor that many other sweeteners lose when heated, but it also needs an additional sweetener in most cases when making baked goods since it doesn't caramelize or create "bulk."

BENEFITS OF STEVIA

1 **WEIGHT LOSS AND DIABETICS.** It does not affect blood sugar metabolism. This makes it a great tool in weight loss programs, but it is also for diabetics. Stevia creates a hypoglycemic effect and increases glucose tolerance. It significantly decreases plasma glucose levels. In multiple human studies, blood sugar is reduced by 35% 6-8 hours after consumption of a hot water extract of the leaf.

2 **BLOOD PRESSURE.** Stevia extract is a vasodilator agent. Studies show that a mix of hot water and extract from the leaf lowers both systolic and diastolic blood pressure. Several studies demonstrated this hypotensive action (as well as a diuretic action).

3 **ANTI-BACTERIAL/ANTI-YEAST.** Stevia has anti-bacterial properties in that it helps to inhibit the growth and reproduction of harmful bacteria that lead to disease. It helps prevent dental cavities by inhibiting the bacteria Streptococcus mutans that stimulates plaque growth. It also has vasodilatory activity and is effective for various skin issues, such as acne, heat rash, and problems caused by insufficient blood circulation.

4 **CANCER.** Studies have shown it keeps your body in a ketogenic state which can starve the cancer of sugar on which cancer feeds.

ERYTHRITOL

Erythritol is a naturally-derived sugar substitute that looks and tastes very much like sugar, yet has almost no calories. Erythritol has been used in Japan since 1990 in candies, chocolate, yogurt, fillings, jellies, jams, beverages, and as a sugar substitute. Erythritol, is considered a 'sugar alcohol' and is found naturally in small amounts in grapes, melons, mushrooms, and fermented foods such as wine, beer, cheese, and soy sauce. Erythritol is usually made from plant sugars. Sugar is mixed with water and then fermented with a natural culture into erythritol. It is then filtered, allowed to crystallize, and then dried. The finished product is white granules or powder that resembles sugar.

CALORIES	0 to 0.2 calories/gram (95% fewer calories than sugar)
SWEETNESS	70% as sweet as table sugar. Use cup for cup like sugar and add a tsp of stevia glycerite to add sweetness.

BENEFITS OF ERYTHRITOL

1 IT HAS A CRYSTALLIZATION PROPERTY LIKE SUGAR. This is why you can't just use stevia for baking.

2 WEIGHT LOSS AND DIABETES. Erythritol does not affect blood glucose or insulin levels.

3 ORAL HEALTH. Erythritol isn't metabolized by oral bacteria which break down sugars and starches to produce acids, which means that it doesn't contribute to tooth decay. This is why excess carbohydrates and table sugar lead to tooth enamel loss and cavities formation.

4 CANDIDA. Erythritol is absorbed in the small intestines, which reduces fermentation and decreases the detrimental problems associated with Candida (yeast overgrowth in the body).

UNDESIRED PROPERTIES: It doesn't dissolve in foods (like salad dressings/caramel)

NAME BRANDS OF STEVIA-ERYTHRITOL BLENDS

1 TRUVIA. Coca-Cola brand. It is expensive and I don't enjoy opening a million little packets if the store doesn't carry the tubs. This is why I purchase erythritol and stevia glycerite separate.

2 ZSWEET. It comes in convenient large bags (as compared to the small tubs of Truvia). A lot of people prefer the taste of ZSweet over other non-caloric sweeteners.

3 ORGANIC ZERO. Is produced from Organic Sugar Cane Juice, which is naturally fermented and crystallized to create Organic Erythritol. Organic Zero is 70% as sweet as table sugar. So you need to add 1 tsp of stevia when using it in your baked goods.

XYLITOL

Xylitol occurs naturally in many fruits and vegetables and is even produced by the human body during normal metabolism. Manufacturers make it from plants such as birch and other hard wood trees and fibrous vegetation. Some people prefer the taste of xylitol. I only use it when I have to since it has a higher calorie content and causes an increase in insulin. Before I found JUST LIKE SUGAR, I used this for my caramel sauce.

CALORIES	2.4 calories/gram; 1 tsp has 9.6 calories and 1 tsp of sugar has 15 calories (40% fewer calories and 75% fewer carbs than table sugar)
SWEETNESS/ CONVERSION	Same as table sugar. Use cup for cup.

BENEFITS OF XYLITOL

1 40% fewer calories than sugar.

2 Researchers found that kids who consistently chewed Xylitol gum had 40% fewer ear infections than those who did not.

3 Pregnant women benefit from Xylitol to keep their teeth healthy especially during the third trimester, when teeth are especially soft.

4 Eating Xylitol gum or mints stimulates saliva flow. This will protect your teeth because it brings the PH levels close to neutral. (diet soda has a pH 2.2)

5 Reduces tooth decay: If you drink acidic sports drinks frequently, eat carbohydrates often and spend hours dehydrated and breathing through a dry acidic mouth, such as athletes and teenagers do, these are risk factors for tooth decay. Stidues have shown Xylitol may help.

6 Studies show that a consistent use of at least 6-8 grams of Xylitol daily can reduce cavities as much as 80%. If you already have gum disease or cavities, these problems can be reversed. Regular use of Xylitol can stop things from getting worse (along with a grain-free diet and increased consumption of fat soluble vitamins A, D, E and K).

UNDESIRED PROPERTIES: Xylitol has very few known side effects, although some people report diarrhea when adding xylitol into their diets. Note: Xylitol is fatal to animals...don't let your dog get a piece of sugar-free gum!

NATURE'S HOLLOW PRODUCTS are made with xylitol: honey, pancake syrup, jelly, BBQ sauce, Ketchup

SWERVE

Swerve is a great tasting, natural sweetener that measures cup-for-cup just like sugar! Made from a unique combination of non-GMO ingredients derived from fruits and vegetables, Swerve contains no artificial ingredients, preservatives or flavors. Swerve is non-glycemic and safe for those living with diabetes. Human clinical trials have shown that Swerve does not affect blood glucose or insulin levels.

CALORIES	0
SWEETNESS	Same as table sugar. Use cup for cup.

The secret to our zero calorie sweetness is a combination of erythritol and oligosaccharides that provide excellent baking and cooking functionality. And with the ability to brown and caramelize, Swerve is gonna be right at home in your kitchen.

JUST LIKE SUGAR

Made from chicory root, calcium, vitamin C, natural flavor, orange peel.

CALORIES	0
SWEETNESS	Same as table sugar. Use cup for cup.

Just Like Sugar has none of the strong aftertastes of stevia or artificial sweeteners. It also keeps ice cream soft, makes perfect caramel sauce, makes cookies soft on the inside and chewy on the outside, and it tastes great.

BENEFITS OF CHICORY ROOT
(Oligosaccharides)

1 **CHOLESTEROL.** Studies suggest it decreases the levels of serum LDL cholesterol in the blood.

2 **INFLAMMATION.** It contains vitamin C, one of the most powerful antioxidants.

3 **DIABETES.** The inulin content is not digestible, so its lack of glucose can help promote optimal blood sugar levels while also increasing stool bulk and consistency.

4 **CONSTIPATION.** It provides soluble fiber, which improves digestion.

5 **GALL BLADDER ISSUES.** Studies show it can builds your body's resistance to gallstones and liver stones. By increasing the flow of bile, it assists the body in digesting foods and liquids. The extra bile also helps break down fats in the body. Chicory root has a mild laxative effect, increases bile from the gallbladder, and decreases swelling.

6 **URINARY INFECTIONS, KIDNEY STONES AND GOUT.** It has diuretic properties that provide protection for the urinary tract system and kidneys. Toxins are removed and the cleansing of the body is stimulated because of an increase in urine flow. It has been used to expel gravel, calcium deposits, and excess uric acid from the body, which helps to prevent gout and kidney stones.

7 **WEIGHT LOSS.** Studies have also shown that chicory root can benefit weight loss because of the effect it has on the digestive system. It is an excellent source of fructooligosaccharides which help promote the growth of beneficial bacteria in your digestive tract. It also increases the rate of the breakdown of fats. It also helps with weight loss because it helps keep insulin levels low while enjoying sweet foods.

8 **NATURAL "LIVER" CLEANSER.** Chicory root also supports the body's detoxification system through the liver and kidneys, and is believed to help with calcium absorption. Chicory may also help prevent jaundice and an enlarged liver when mixed with water. Because of Chicory Root's potential for removing contaminants from the digestive system, the liver does not have to work as hard to filter out toxins that may have escaped into the bloodstream. It also acts as a

gentle laxative and diuretic for removing excess water and toxins, and this can also reduce strain on the liver.

9 ANXIETY. It is a natural sedative and anti-inflammatory for the nervous system. If you have anxiety issues and still drink coffee, this sweetener may help.

10 INDIGESTION. It can act as an herbal antacid; the root neutralizes acid and corrects acid indigestion, heartburn, gastritis, vomiting and upset stomach. Because it stimulates bile production, this helps to speed up the digestive process after eating too much rich food.

11 SKIN. Used externally, the Chicory Root has been shown to have healing properties for cuts, sunburn, swellings, hemorrhoids, and poison ivy. It reduces the inflammation of rheumatism and the pain of sore joints.

UNDESIRED PROPERTIES: It is expensive, but other than that it is perfect! **NOTE:** it is 96 grams of fiber/cup; if you add this to a liquid it will gel up.

ALLERGENS: If you are allergic to ragweed, you may be allergic to the Chicory Root.

CHOCOPERFECTION Chocolate Bars are sweetened with Chicory Root and are my favorite chocolate for baking.

Glycemic Index of Sweeteners

Sweetener	GI
Stevia Glycerite	0
Erythritol	0
Truvia/ZSWEET	0
Swerve	0
JUST LIKE SUGAR	0
Xylitol	7
Maple Syrup	54
Honey	62
Table Sugar	68
Splenda	80
High Fructose Corn Syrup	87

WHERE TO FIND THESE INGREDIENTS

Some of my specific ingredients are hard to find (or really expensive in grocery stores). I created an online 'store' where you can find these ingredients at the best prices I have found. For easy online shopping go to:

http://astore.amazon.com/marisnutran05-20

The more sugar we eat, the more we crave it. If you start your day off with cereal and skim milk, you aren't going to be able to walk by the candy jar in your office at 2pm! Check out these to breakfast comparisons:

Option 1:
- 1 cup SMART START Cereal
- 1 cup skim milk
- banana

472 calories, 105 carbs, 4g fiber = 25.25 tsp of sugar in blood (IF you didn't add any sugar!)

Option 2:
- 2 eggs,
- 2 cups of mushrooms, peppers, onions

190 calories, 9 carbs, 3 fiber = 1.5 tsp of sugar in blood

Option 3:
- My homemade donut made with coconut flour

217 calories, 7.4 carbs, 4.6g fiber = 0.7 tsp of sugar in blood!

To eat is a necessity; to eat 'healthy' is an art.

Sweetener Conversion

My recipes call for using Swerve (granular or confectioners, they are both equal) wherever sweetener is needed. I find this gives the best overall results when baking and cooking. If a specific natural sweetener is called for (like xylitol or Just Like Sugar) then substitutions are not allowed. For some recipes (where the sweetener has to melt for instance) some sweeteners won't work. In any recipe that lists "Swerve (or equivalent)" you can use ZSweet, Truvia, Organic Zero, Xylitol or Just Like Sugar. In order to use a different product, use this chart to convert.

1 cup Swerve	=	1 cup erythritol and 1 tsp stevia glycerite
1 cup Swerve	=	1 cup Organic Zero and 1 tsp stevia glycerite
1 cup Swerve	=	1 cup Truvia
1 cup Swerve	=	1 cup Xylitol
1 cup Swerve	=	1 cup Just Like Sugar

Why Whey Protein

TIP

When buying a whey protein product, "Whey Protein Isolate" is the highest quality you can buy; which has at least 90% protein with only trace amounts of fat and lactose. Also check the sugar count; some brands add way too much sugar to make whey taste like candy and get you hooked on their product… and that sugar isn't going to help our waist line!

Did you know that if you gain 10 pounds of muscle, you will burn an extra 3500 calories per week? To burn that many calories doing cardio, you would have to run for an hour each day of the week! To build 10 pounds of muscle, feed your body a high quality whey protein 1-3 times a day, and increase strength training. Whey protein is my favorite addition to my diet in the past few years.

Top 10 REASONS to Consume Whey

1 BOOST IMMUNE SYSTEM. Whey protein includes high levels of the amino acid cysteine, which produces glutathione, a potent antioxidant that maintains immune health. One of the first indications in patients with autoimmune diseases is a decrease in glutathione levels. Many studies have proven adding whey protein to patients with chronic fatigue syndrome, cancer, and HIV can greatly enhance their immune system. Scientists discovered that whey proteins stopped the growth of breast cancer cells in test tubes. It was also proven that when patients ingest at least 24 grams of whey a day they had a noteworthy reduction in the size of cancer tumors.

2 ENHANCE INFANT FORMULA. Whey protein contains alpha-lactalbumin and is the main nutrient in human breast milk. This makes whey protein a very important nutrient to include in infant formulas and should be the first protein consumed by babies. Good news to mothers; the Journal of Pediatrics found that formulas with whey protein have been shown to help reduce the length of crying spells in babies with colic. Not all contain whey because it costs more.

3 BENEFIT CARDIOVASCULAR HEALTH. Adding whey along with your doctor's prescription can be a great balance to help your heart. Clinical research discovered that whey protein reduces blood pressure in individuals who are borderline hypertensive.

4 INCREASE LEAN BODY MASS. Our muscles need branched chain amino acids (BCAAs) during long periods of exercise and added stress, which can also have a negative effect on the immune system. Whey proteins are naturally high in BCAAs that are easy to digest. It immediately

supplies the muscles with the high quality protein it is screaming for, which directly correlates to an increase in physical performance and enhanced body composition.

5 CONTRIBUTE TO A POSITIVE MOOD. Stress is a well-known cause of a decrease in serotonin levels in the brain, which can cause depression. Clinical studies found that including whey protein is helpful in enhancing moods and in boosting serotonin levels because it is high in tryptophan, a natural relaxant. Whey is great for people with high stress lifestyles and elevated cortisol hormones.

6 SUPERIOR PROTEIN SOURCE FOR LACTOSE, CASEIN OR GLUTEN FREE DIETS. Whey protein isolate is the purest form and is over 90% protein. Whey protein isolate contains only trace amounts of lactose, therefore people with lactose allergies can safely enjoy whey. It is also a great protein source for people with Celiac disease who are on gluten or wheat protein-restricted diets.

7 AN APPETITE SUPPRESSOR. One of the nutrients in whey protein, glycomacropeptide, stimulates the release of cholecystokinin, which is an appetite suppressing hormone.

8 STAVE OFF OSTEOPOROSIS. Osteoporosis affects over 25 million Americans. We have the highest rate of hip fractures, yet we have the highest intake of calcium in the world, next to Sweden. Studies show that low protein intake, including low levels of animal protein consumption, was directly related to increased levels of bone loss. Impact exercise, such as walking, and sufficient amounts of protein in the diet can enhance bone health and may help to reduce the frequency of osteoporosis.

9 HELP PROTECT AGAINST ULCERS AND ACID REFLUX. Lactoferrin, a nutrient in whey protein, is a known inhibitor of many forms of bacteria that is responsible for digestive problems; such as gastritis and ulcers. In addition, recent animal studies show promising results that it also kills the bacteria responsible for acid reflux.

10 AID WOUND HEALING. People who have burns or are recovering from surgery require additional protein in their diet. Exciting new studies indicate whey protein nutrients promote the growth of new body tissue.

Jay Robb is a superior weight loss brand that uses stevia to sweeten their whey and also use whey sourced from grass fed cows not treated with rBGH (Growth Hormone).

I'm not one to "drink" my calories...I like to eat! So, I use whey in many of my recipes.

Specific Ingredients

Many everyday food ingredients are very high in sugar and carbs. These tables show the various substitutions I use in my recipes. Use this chart to understand the healthier alternatives and why I have selected various ingredients.

MASH POTATOES Substitute: Cauliflower for potatoes

Steam some fresh or frozen cauliflower. Then add a dash of butter to the cauliflower, add a little chicken broth or heavy cream, and puree in a food processor or blender. To make it even better, try adding roasted garlic, cheese, or sour cream to the mixture. If you are apprehensive about your family liking this, just substitute ½ the potatoes for cauliflower the first time and see if anyone says anything!

Carbohydrates Eliminated: 30 g per cup
The Taste Test: "After a couple of bites, you forget it's not potatoes."

Potato Substitutions (Per Cup)					
Item	Rating	Carbs	Sugars	Fiber	Calories
Potato	Bad	28	2	4	116
Sweet Potato	Bad	27	6	4	114
Kamucha Squash (NOT Butternut)	OK	7	3	1	30
Pumpkin (for sweet potato)	OK	7.5	1.6	0.6	30
Turnips	OK	8	5	2	36
Jicama	OK	11	2	6	46
Daikon Radish	Best	2	0	0.5	30
Cauliflower	Best	3	1	1	28

RICE Substitute: Cauliflower Rice instead of white rice

Process fresh cauliflower with a food processor until it is the size of rice. Pan fry the "rice" in a dash of butter. Don't add water, cauliflower absorbs water like crazy, and the "granules" will become gummy. To keep it fluffy, just let the moisture in the cauliflower do its work. Great for Mexican dishes, Asian dishes…Kids even like it.

Carbs Eliminated: 32 g per cup
The Taste: "Awesome, I like it better than white rice!

Rice Substitutions (Per Cup)					
Item	Rating	Carbs	Sugars	Fiber	Calories
White Rice	Bad	53	0	0	242
Brown Rice	Bad	46	0	4	218
Quinoa	Bad	39	0	5	222
Wild Rice	Bad	35	1.2	3	166
Cauliflower Rice	Best	3	1	1	28

PASTA Substitute: Spaghetti squash for spaghetti OR Fresh Shredded ZUCCHINI

Cooked spaghetti squash is Mother Nature's spaghetti. Squash has a flesh that has noodle-like strands. Cut the squash in half and remove the seeds. Then place each half (cut side down) on a plate with a quarter cup of water. Microwave the squash for 8 to 10 minutes or until it's soft to the touch. Let it cool, then scrape out the "spaghetti" strands and top with low sugar marinara sauce and cheese.

Carbohydrates Eliminated: Squash = 30 g per cup! Zucchini = 40 g per cup!

The Taste Test: "Great. Spaghetti squash has exactly the same consistency as real pasta."

Pasta Substitutions (Per Cup)

Item	Rating	Carbs	Sugars	Fiber	Calories
White Pasta	Bad	43	0	5	246
Spaghetti Squash	OK	10	4	2	42
Bean Sprouts	Best	6	4	2	31
Artichoke Hearts	Best	6	0	4	40
Cabbage Noodles	Best	5	3	2	22
Eggplant (lasagna noodles)	Best	5	2	3	20
Zucchini Noodles	Best	4	2	1	20
Sheritaki Tofu Noodles	Best	3	0	2	20
Shaved Deli Meat (lasagna)	Best	0	0	0	30

BAKING Substitutes: Almond, Peanut or Coconut Flour

In my family we treat corn, carrots, potatoes and rice as starchy foods, as if they were sweets (starch and sugar = excess weight gain). They are all starchy carbohydrates as are the products made from them (chips, cereal, rice cakes and snacks). So we never use alternative flours made from corn, rice or potatoes.

4 grams of carbohydrates from sugar or starch becomes 1 teaspoon of sugar in our body!

Flour Substitutions (Per Cup)

Item	Rating	Carbs	Sugars	Fiber	Calories
Rice Flour (Gluten-Free)	Bad	127	0.2	3.8	578
White Flour	Bad	100	0	4	496
Wheat Flour	Bad	87	0	14	407
Oat Flour	Bad	78	0	12	480
Almond Flour	Best	24	4	12	640
Peanut Flour	Best	21	4	9	196
Coconut Flour	Best	80	0	48	480
Flaxseed Meal	Best	32	0	32	480
Psyllium Husk	Best	80	0	72	280
Whey/Egg White Protein	Best	1	0	0	440

Plan Plan Plan = Success
Freezing Meals

I am a working mom of 2 toddler boys and healthy eating is a priority to me. Making food at home is important for so many reasons. For one, you are in control all of the ingredients to make them as healthy as you can! Choosing sauces and mixes without any hydrogenated oils, high fructose corn syrup, artificial colors, gluten or sweeteners.

So here are my tips:

1 Make a list of "healthified" slow cooker recipes that you want to try.

2 Make an ingredient list and shop! Make sure freezer bags and labels are on the list.

3 Lay out ingredients for the recipes you want to prepare.

4 Label your bags with the name of the dish, date and any further directions needed.

5 Clean, chop and prepare the vegetable. Dice onions, peppers, and roast or mince garlic.

6 Add your meats and proteins to the freezer bags, top with veggies and then other ingredients like sauces.

7 Press out any air, seal bag, and lay flat.

8 Freeze & relax!

Better yet, double the recipes you love and have 2 weeks worth of meals!

Pull the bags out of the freezer the night before you want to use them so they're thawed when they go in the slow cooker! And again, rejoice that you don't have another huge mess to clean up!

Each recipe gave me TWO gallon size bags. Each bag is enough to feed my family of 3 (two adults and a toddler) at least one dinner, and at least two lunches, but possibly more.

Slow Cooker Tips

1 If a recipe calls for browning or searing meat, do this the night before. My husband is the best helper and he helps clean up dinner while I prepare dinner for the next night. Even if I will be doing slow cooker meals the next day, I prepare the meat the night before, fill the slow cooker shells and place them in the fridge. All I have to do is take them out of the fridge in the morning and turn them on. Easy as pie!

2 Prepare cauliflower "rice" the night before by pulsing the cauliflower in a food processor until small pieces of "rice." All you have to do is stir fry the

"rice" in a little butter just before serving your slow cooker meal over it.

3 Cook grass fed cuts of meat on a LOW setting. The lower and slower the heat, the less "gamey" it will taste.

4 Bake and store "Healthified" Protein Bread, Buns, Tortillas and other gluten free and low carb breads in the freezer for easy additions to your slow cooker meal. I always have Pesto Rolls, Protein Buns and Tomato Basil Tortillas in my freezer.

19

Gingerbread Latte

Ingredients:

4 c. unsweetened almond milk

½ c. Swerve, Granular (or equivalent)

2 tsp ground ginger

2 tsp vanilla extract

1 tsp ground cinnamon

¼ tsp cloves

¼ tsp nutmeg

Optional Garnish:

cinnamon sticks

whipped cream

Makes 4 servings

Directions:

1　Place the almond milk, natural sweetener and spices in a 2-quart slow cooker.

2　Cover and cook on low for 3 hours. Don't boil.

3　Pour over hot organic coffee or espresso.

4　Garnish with cinnamon sticks, whipped cream, a sprinkle of nutmeg.

Nutritional Comparison:

Item	Calories	Fat	Protein	Carbs	Fiber	Effective Carbs
Traditional Latte	254	9g	6g	42g	0g	42g
"Healthified" Latte	35	0g	2g	1g	0g	1g

Hot Chocolate

Ingredients:

2 oz. (2 squares) unsweetened chocolate

⅓ c. Swerve, Granular (or equivalent)

4 c. unsweetened almond milk or coconut milk

½ tsp Celtic sea salt

½ tsp vanilla

Makes 4 servings

Directions:

1　Place chocolate, natural sweetener, almond milk, and salt in a 2-quart slow cooker over medium-low heat for 1-4 hours.

2　Heat, stirring, until chocolate melts and mixture is well blended.

3　Add vanilla and serve.

Nutritional Comparison (per serving):

Item	Calories	Fat	Protein	Carbs	Fiber	Effective Carbs
Traditional Hot Chocolate	283	15.3g	9g	32g	2.3g	29.7g
"Healthified" Hot Chocolate	113	10g	3g	6.3g	3.4g	2.9g

Ginger Ale

Ingredients:

1 lb fresh ginger, unpeeled and
    cut in a small dice

2 lemons, juiced (reserve peel)

1 ½ c. Swerve, Granular
    (or equivalent)

1- quart Carbonated water

Garnish: lime wedges

Directions:

1   Combine the ginger and lemon juice in a food processor and process until minced, stopping the machine periodically and scraping down the sides, if necessary.

2   Place the puree in a slow cooker with the natural sweetener and 1-quart water. Add the lemon peel to the pot. Cook on high heat for 4-8 hours (the longer the better). Turn off the heat. Cool, then strain and chill.

3   To serve, place about 2 TBS of the ginger mixture in a glass full of ice. Fill with carbonated water; taste and add more ginger mix if you like. Garnish with a lime wedge, then serve.

Nutritional Comparison:

Item	Calories	Fat	Protein	Carbs	Fiber	Effective Carbs
Traditional Ginger Ale	124	0g	0g	32.1g	0g	32.1g
"Healthified" Ginger Ale	49	0g	1.3g	9g	2g	7g

Makes 32 servings

Benefits of Ginger

1 **PROBLEMS WITH MINERAL ABSORPTION?** This is a common problem with people who have gluten sensitivities and celiac. Ginger improves the absorption and assimilation of essential nutrients in the body.

2 **INDIGESTION.** Ginger increases the production of digestive juices.

3 **SINUS ISSUES.** Ginger clears the sinuses 'microcirculatory channels' in the body that flare up from time to time.

4 **GINGER HEALS DECREASE NAUSEA AND TUMMY CRAMPS.** This is often another downside of surgery; chewing ginger post-operation can help overcome nausea.

5 **GAS.** Ginger helps reduce flatulence.

6 **JOINT PAIN.** Ginger has anti-inflammatory properties. Rub ginger essential oil onto aching muscles and joints.

7 **CONGESTION.** Stir up some ginger tea to get rid of throat and nose congestion.

8 **LIBIDO.** Ginger has aphrodisiac properties.

Cereal

Ingredients:

⅓ c. Swerve, Granular (or equivalent)

⅓ c. crushed almonds/pecans/walnuts

¼ c. almond flour

¼ c. JAY ROBB vanilla whey protein (or egg white protein)

¼ c. butter or coconut oil, softened

1 tsp pure organic blueberry extract

1 tsp cinnamon

Directions:

1 In a large bowl, stir all the ingredients together. Place in a 4-quart slow cooker.

2 Cover and cook on low for 2-3 hours or until the butter is melted and nuts are a bit toasted (it will still be soft, but once it cools, it crisps up).

3 Pour onto a piece of parchment to cool. It will crisp up once completely cool.

4 NOTE: if you use coconut oil, this is 'shelf stable' and doesn't need refrigeration. Perfect for family outings and vacations! Serve with unsweetened vanilla almond milk.

Nutritional Comparison (per serving):

Item	Calories	Fat	Protein	Carbs	Fiber	Effective Carbs
Post Cereal	220	3g	3g	45g	2g	43g
"Healthified" Cereal	220	9.2g	18g	4g	2g	2g

Milk Comparison (per cup):

Item	Calories	Carbs	Sugar	Effective Carbs
Skim Milk	90	13g	13g	13g
Unsweetened Almond Milk	35	1g	0g	1g

Makes 4 servings

Granola

Ingredients:

2 c. chopped pecans

½ c. chopped walnuts

½ c. slivered almonds

1 c. sunflower seeds

1 ¾ c. Jay Robb vanilla whey or egg white protein

½ c. sesame seeds

1 ¼ c. coconut oil or butter

½ c. Swerve, Granular (or equivalent)

1 tsp cinnamon

½ tsp Celtic sea salt

Directions:

1 In a large bowl, stir all the ingredients together. Place in a 4-quart slow cooker.

2 Cover and cook on low for 2-3 hours or until the butter is melted and nuts are a bit toasted (it will still be soft, but once it cools, it crisps up).

3 Pour onto a piece of parchment to cool. It will crisp up once completely cool.

4 NOTE: if you use coconut oil, this is 'shelf stable' and doesn't need refrigeration. Perfect for family outings and vacations!

5 Serve with unsweetened vanilla almond milk.

Nutritional Comparison (¼ cup serving):

Item	Calories	Fat	Protein	Carbs	Fiber	Effective Carbs
BareNaked Granola	130	2.5g	4g	22g	2g	20g
"Healthified" Granola	130	8g	5.3g	2.3g	0.9g	1.4g

Makes 48 ¼ cup servings

Overnight "Oat"meal

Ingredients:

3 ½ c. unsweetened vanilla or
    chocolate almond milk

8 TBS freshly ground golden flax
    seeds (or more for thicker)

6 tsp psyllium husk

1 c. vanilla or chocolate egg
    white/whey protein

1 TBS vanilla extract

1 drop of stevia glycerite
    (or natural sweetener to taste)

½ tsp of nutmeg

½ tsp cinnamon

OPTIONAL:

You can add some coconut flakes,
nuts or peanut butter to this recipe.

Directions:

1   Combine all ingredients (and optional ingredients) in a 4-quart slow cooker.

2   Stir well and let sit on low overnight for the flavors to meld and until the "oatmeal" thickens. Enjoy!

TIP: You can't hide a lot of super-healthy foods...I don't think I could disguise salmon in an ice cream and my nephew will never try "KALE CHIPS" again:) But flax seeds have an agreeable flavor and texture for kids. Flax seeds are great sources of omega-3s (proven to help with improved learning capacity as well as many other health benefits), they are also affordable and tasty. Flax is important because it contains lignans that have been shown to be effective for cancer treatment. It also aids immune health, fights inflammation and is great for brain health. This breakfast is also helpful for constipation.

Nutritional Comparison (per serving):

Item	Calories	Fat	Protein	Carbs	Fiber	Effective Carbs
Traditional Oatmeal with Skim Milk	269	3.7g	13.4g	46g	5g	41g
"Healthified" "Oat" meal	254	10g	22g	18g	13.6g	4.4g

Makes 4 servings

French Toast Casserole

Ingredients:

PROTEIN BREAD:

1 ¼ c. blanched almond flour
   (or ½ cup coconut flour)

4 TBS psyllium husk powder

2 tsp baking powder

1 tsp Celtic sea salt

3 egg whites (8 egg whites if using
   coconut flour)

1 c. BOILING water

EGG MIXTURE:

2 whole eggs

2 egg whites

1 ½ c. unsweetened almond or
   coconut milk

¼ c. Swerve, Granular (or equivalent)

1 tsp pure vanilla extract

½ tsp cinnamon

9 Slices Protein Bread

FILLING:

1 c. peeled zucchini, sliced in thin
   "apple" slices

3 TBS Swerve, Granular
   (or equivalent)

1 TBS lemon juice

⅓ c. raw pecans, diced

½ tsp cinnamon

Makes 9 servings

Directions:

1 Preheat the oven to 350 degrees F.

2 In a medium sized bowl, combine the flour, psyllium powder (no substitutes: flaxseed meal won't work), baking powder and salt. Mix until dry ingredients are well combined. Add in the eggs and mix until a thick dough. Add boiling water in the bowl. Mix until well combined and dough firms up.

3 Form in a long subs (like a loaf of French bread) and place onto a greased baking sheet. Bake for 65 minutes. Remove from the oven and allow the bread cool completely. Cut in slices. You will only use about ½ the loaf.

4 Grease a 6-quart slow cooker.

5 In a medium bowl, combine the eggs, egg whites, unsweetened almond milk, natural sweetener, vanilla and cinnamon. Add all the filling ingredients to the bowl and stir to coat zucchini pieces, set aside.

6 Cut Protein bread slices in triangles (that's in half, just triangle shaped). Place one layer of bread (6 triangles) on the bottom of the slow cooker, add ¼ of the filling and repeat until there are 3 layers of bread. Add the remaining filling to the top. Pour egg mixture over bread.

7 Cover and cook on high 2 to 2-½ or low 4 hours, or until bread has soaked up the liquid.

OPTIONAL: drizzle with xylitol "maple" syrup (like Nature's Hollow) if desired.

Nutritional Comparison (per serving):

Item	Calories	Fat	Protein	Carbs	Fiber	Effective Carbs
Traditional Casserole	198	9g	4g	30.4g	1.8g	28.6g
"Healthified" Casserole	122	8.6g	6g	6g	3.8g	2.2g

Coffee Cake

Ingredients:

CAKE:

4 c. blanched almond flour
    (OR 1 cup coconut flour)

1 TBS baking powder

1 tsp cinnamon

¾ tsp Celtic sea salt

⅔ c. butter or coconut oil

1 ⅓ c. Swerve, Granular
    (or equivalent)

1 ½ tsp vanilla extract

3 eggs (6 eggs if using coconut flour)

⅔ c. unsweetened almond milk

CINNAMON SYRUP:

½ c. Swerve, Confectioners
    (or equivalent)

6 TBS butter

⅓ c. water

1 tsp vanilla extract

3 tsp ground cinnamon

CREAM CHEESE LAYER:

8 oz. cream cheese or coconut cream
    (if dairy allergy)

¼ c. unsweetened vanilla almond milk

¼ c. Swerve, Granular
    (or equivalent to taste)

Makes 14 servings

Directions:

1   Grease a 4-quart slow cooker. Cut a piece of parchment paper to fit the bottom of the stoneware and press in place and grease well.

2   Blend all cake ingredients in a large bowl until well blended. Spoon batter in slow cooker.

3   Mix the cinnamon syrup ingredients in a small bowl and spoon mixture on top of cake.

4   Cover and cook on low for 3 to 4 hours or until toothpick inserted in center comes out clean.

5   Let cake rest 10 minutes and then invert onto plate, peel off parchment paper. Then invert again onto serving platter. Once cool, drizzle frosting over the top.

6   **CREAM CHEESE FROSTING:** beat cream cheese with ¼ cup vanilla almond milk and natural sweetener (to taste). You can make this ahead of time and store in the fridge (it will get thicker overnight). Dollop a tablespoon or two on top of cake.

Nutritional Comparison (per serving):

Item	Calories	Fat	Protein	Carbs	Fiber	Effective Carbs
Traditional Cinnamon Cake	390	10g	4g	72g	1g	71g
"Healthified" Almond Flour Cake	387	35g	9.5g	8g	3.5g	4.5g
"Healthified" Coconut Flour Cake	254	22g	5.5g	5.8g	2.9g	2.9g

Glazed Breakfast Cake

Ingredients:

STREUSEL TOPPING:

¼ c. blanched almond flour

¼ c. Swerve, Granular (or equivalent)

2 TBS coconut oil or butter

½ tsp cinnamon

BATTER:

1 ½ c. blanched almond flour

¾ c. Swerve, Granular (or equivalent)

½ c. plain Greek yogurt or
   coconut milk

1 large egg, lightly beaten

1 tsp vanilla or almond extract

GLAZE:

3 TBS unsweetened almond
   milk plus a little more

½ c. Swerve, Confectioners
   (or equivalent)

Directions:

1 Grease a 2-quart slow cooker. Cut a piece of parchment paper to fit the bottom of the stoneware and grease well.

2 In a small bowl, mix the streusel ingredients and set aside. In a medium bowl, mix the batter ingredients until well blended. Spoon ½ batter in slow cooker. Sprinkle ½ streusel mixture on top and then repeat with remaining batter and streusel.

3 In a small bowl, whisk almond milk and natural sweetener until slightly runny in consistency and set aside.

4 Cover and cook on low for 3 to 4 hours or until toothpick inserted in center comes out clean.

5 Let cake rest 10 minutes and then invert onto plate, peel off parchment paper. Then invert again onto serving platter. Once cool, spoon glaze over top.

Nutritional Comparison (per serving):

Item	Calories	Fat	Protein	Carbs	Fiber	Effective Carbs
Traditional Breakfast Cake	323	20g	3g	32g	0g	32g
"Healthified" Breakfast Cake	131	10g	4.6g	4.3g	1.6g	2.7g

Makes 12 servings

Crust-less Quiche

Ingredients:

4 slices bacon

1 TBS butter or coconut oil

2 c. coarsely chopped portobello
    mushrooms

½ c. red sweet pepper, chopped

8 eggs

1 ½ c. shredded Gruyère cheese
    or Swiss cheese

1 c. unsweetened almond milk

2 TBS snipped fresh chives

½ tsp Celtic sea salt

¼ tsp ground black pepper

2 TBS coconut flour

Directions:

1   Line a 3-½- or 4-quart slow cooker with parchment paper and grease
    well.

2   In a medium skillet cook bacon until crisp; drain, crumble, and set
    aside. Discard drippings. In same skillet heat oil over medium heat.
    Add mushrooms and sweet pepper; cook and stir until tender.

3   In a medium bowl combine eggs, cheese. unsweetened almond milk
    (make sure it isn't vanilla), chives, salt, and black pepper. Stir egg mix-
    ture with the vegetables in skillet. Blend in coconut flour. Pour egg
    mixture in prepared slow cooker. Sprinkle with bacon.

4   Cover and cook on low for 4 to 5 hours or until a knife inserted in the
    center comes out clean. Turn off cooker. Remove from slow cooker.
    Cool for 15 to 30 minutes before serving.

Nutritional Comparison (per serving):

Item	Calories	Fat	Protein	Carbs	Fiber	Effective Carbs
Traditional Quiche	333	19.4g	13g	25.3g	1g	24.3g
"Healthified" Quiche	173	12.1g	12g	4.2g	1.2g	3g

Makes 8 servings

Hard Boiled Eggs

Ingredients:

12 eggs

Directions:

1 Place the eggs in slow cooker. Cover with water. Cover and cook on low for 3 ½ hours.

Nutritional Comparison (per serving):

Item	Calories	Fat	Protein	Carbs	Fiber	Effective Carbs
"Healthified" Eggs	70	5g	7g	0.5g	0g	0.5g

Makes 12 servings

Easy Homemade Ricotta

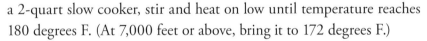

Ingredients:

3 c. organic whole milk

1 c. organic heavy cream

½ tsp Celtic sea salt

3 TBS fresh squeezed lemon juice

Directions:

1 Place the milk, cream and salt in a 2-quart slow cooker, stir and heat on low until temperature reaches 180 degrees F. (At 7,000 feet or above, bring it to 172 degrees F.)

2 Once the temperature has reached 180 degrees, remove from heat, stir in the lemon juice, cover and set aside in a warm place (80 - 100 degrees F) for 6 hours.

3 The ricotta is ready to strain when a solid curd has formed. Strain through several layers of damp cheese cloth or a fine metal strainer; discard the whey (the watery residue).

Nutritional Comparison (per serving):

Item	Calories	Fat	Protein	Carbs	Fiber	Effective Carbs
Traditional Ricotta	113	8.5g	3.3g	6g	trace	6g
"Healthified" Ricotta	108	8.5g	3.3g	5g	trace	5g

Makes 8 servings

Bran Muffins

Ingredients:

1 ½ c. ALMOND bran

1 c. unsweetened almond milk

⅓ c. coconut oil or butter

1 egg (3 if using coconut flour)

⅔ c. Swerve, Granular
    (or equivalent)

½ tsp pure vanilla extract

1 c. blanched almond flour
    (or ¼ cup coconut flour)

1 tsp baking soda

1 tsp baking powder

½ tsp Celtic sea salt

1 tsp cinnamon (if desired)

Directions:

1   Grease tea cups or line with paper muffin liners.

2   Mix together almond bran and almond milk; let stand for 10 minutes. Beat together oil, egg, natural sweetener (*NOTE: if using Just Like Brown Sugar, I suggest to add 1 tsp of stevia glycerite for a better sweet flavor) and vanilla and add to bran mixture.

3   Sift together almond flour, baking soda, baking powder and salt (and cinnamon if desired). Stir flour mixture in bran mixture, until just blended.

4   Place the dough in cute greased tea cups. Place the tea cups in the largest slow cooker you own. Place water in the slow cooker to fill ⅔ of the way up the tea cups (making sure not to get water in the cups).

5   Cover and cook on low for 2 to 4 hours. To check if done, insert a clean toothpick in the center and when you remove the toothpick, when it comes out clean, it is baked through. Remove from slow cooker and let cool in for 10 minutes.

6   Top with Nature's Hollow Honey if desired.

Nutritional Comparison (per serving):

Item	Calories	Fat	Protein	Carbs	Fiber	Effective Carbs
Traditional Bran Muffins	167	7.1g	3.5g	25.6g	2.5g	23.1
"Healthified" Almond Flour Bran Muffins	127	11g	4g	3.9g	2.9g	1g
"Healthified" Coconut Bran Muffins	102	7g	3g	3.8g	2.9g	0.9g

Makes 12 servings

A product of Nut-Trition, Inc.
1825 Verduga Road Hughson, CA 95326
For information contact Dr. Sam Cunningham
Phone (916) 804-4525
Or Robert Miltner
Phone (415) 924-7229

Learn about our products at
Nut-Trition.com
Product of U.S.A.

Almond Bran

When I was a teenager I had the best job ever! I worked at a beautiful coffee shop in my home town before and after school. I loved baking and serving yummy muffins and cinnamon rolls to eager customers. The best part was that since we served everything fresh, I was allowed to take home all the leftover muffins.

If I had more time, I would love to open my own cafe with "healthified" mochas and muffins. And these "Bran Muffins" would certainly be on the menu.

Almond bran is a new favorite baking product. There are many health benefits in the outer skin of the almond; which is the "bran" part of the almond.

Almond Bran is 100% almond skin, so there are way less calories and fat (not that I'm afraid of the fat, but then we can add more coconut oil!). There are no man-made vitamins, chemicals or fillers. Almond Bran is just the yummy goodness of almond flavor and nutrition in a concentrated form.

Why do I love almond bran? Almond Bran contains:
- Less than half the fat...so I can add more BUTTER!
- Almost 4 times the fiber
- 4 times the phytosterols
- 20 times the amount of stigmasterol
- 7 times the amount of campesterol

Sweet n Spicy Nuts

Ingredients:

1 c. raw macadamia nuts

1 c. raw pecans

1 c. raw almonds

½ c. raw sunflower seeds

3 TBS xylitol

2 TBS butter or coconut oil

½ tsp Celtic sea salt

FLAVOR PROFILES:

1 tsp garam marsala powder

¼ tsp cayenne pepper

OR:

1 tsp rosemary

¼ tsp tarragon

OR:

1 tsp lemon grass

½ tsp cayenne

Directions:

1 Grease a 4-quart (or larger) slow cooker. Place all the ingredients in the slow cooker and stir until nuts are coated well.

2 Cover and cook on high for 2 hours, stirring every 20 minutes or so or the nuts will burn.

3 Spread the nuts out on a layer of wax paper to cool. Store in an air-tight container or wrap in cute bags and give as gifts.

NOTE: You can mix up with different nuts and spices, but I don't recommend cashews or pistachios; they are too high in starch.

Nutritional Comparison (per serving):

Item	Calories	Fat	Protein	Carbs	Fiber	Effective Carbs
Traditional Spiced Nuts	240	21g	3.8g	11.2g	3g	8.2g
"Healthified" Spiced Nuts	216	21g	3.8g	4.9g	3g	1.9g

Makes 12 servings

Candied Walnuts

Ingredients:

2 TBS coconut oil or butter

2 c. walnut halves

¼ c. xylitol

1 tsp Celtic sea salt

Directions:

1 Place walnuts, butter, natural sweetener and salt in the slow cooker and cook on high for an hour.

2 After an hour, mix the nuts with a wooden spoon.

3 Remove from the slow cooker and spread out on parchment paper, or a few cookie sheets. Allow to cool and they will crisp up as they rest.

Nutritional Comparison (per serving):

Item	Calories	Fat	Protein	Carbs	Fiber	Effective Carbs
Traditional Candied Nuts	250	21g	7.5g	10.1g	2.1g	8g
"Healthified" Candied Nuts	222	21g	7.5g	3.1g	2.1g	1g

Makes 8 servings

MSG

EMERALD DRY ROASTED ALMOND INGREDIENTS: Dry Roasted Almonds, Seasoning (Maltodextrin, Contains 2% or Less of the Following: Salt, Modified Potato Starch, Sugar, Monosodium Glutamate, Paprika, Onion Powder, Autolyzed Yeast Extract, Garlic Powder, Natural Flavor, Modified Corn Starch, Corn Syrup Solids).

MSG (an excitotoxin) causes damage to the neurons in your brain and has links to Parkinson's disease, Alzheimer's, Huntington's disease and many others. Children are very susceptible to this type of effect on their sensitive and growing brains. Excitotoxins excite the neurons in the brain too much. They become exhausted and die. Neurotoxins are also a main cause of seizures . The damage may not be seen until many years later. When this happens, our neurotransmitters responsible for focus, mood, and memory have a hard time finding and recognizing their receptors due to the inflammation of the membranes on the brain cells caused by the consumption of MSG.

I THOUGHT THIS WOULD GET YOUR ATTENTION: Consuming MSG triples the amount of insulin the pancreas creates. Excess insulin = obesity.

Roasted Garlic

Ingredients:

10 garlic bulbs

Directions:

1   Cut the very end of the bulb of garlic off with a sharp knife while keeping the cloves wrapped in the outer layers of the skin.

2   Wrap each bulb in a piece of foil. Place each wrapped bulb in a 2-quart slow cooker and cook on low for 4-5 hours.

3   Unwrap each bulb and squeeze the bulb. If garlic squirts out (like a tube of frosting) it is done. If not, wrap it back up and cook for another hour.

WHY GARLIC? It contains phyto-nutrients that are studies have shown can help fight coronary artery diseases, infections and cancers. Garlic contains allicin, which reduces harmful cholesterol by inhibiting the HMG-CoA reductase enzyme within the liver cells. Allicin also decreases blood vessel stiffness by release of nitric oxide (NO), which lowers blood pressure. Allicin also blocks platelet clot formation and has fibrinolytic action in the blood vessels, which can help decrease the overall risk from heart disease and stroke.

Nutritional Comparison (per serving):

Item	Calories	Fat	Protein	Carbs	Fiber	Effective Carbs
"Healthified" Garlic	15	0g	0g	3g	0g	3g

Makes 10 servings

Marinara Sauce

Ingredients:

1 medium yellow onion

½ TBS minced garlic

6 c. organic tomatoes, crushed

1 (6-oz.) organic tomato paste

1 TBS Swerve, Granular
(or equivalent)

1 TBS coconut or balsamic
vinegar

2 whole bay leaves

1 TBS dried basil

½ TBS dried oregano

Celtic sea salt & pepper, to taste

Directions:

1   Cut the onion in a small dice and mince the garlic and place in a 4-quart slow cooker. Also add the crushed tomatoes, tomato paste, natural sweetener, vinegar, bay leaves, basil, oregano, and freshly cracked pepper. Stir well to combine.

2   Cover and cook on low for at least 8 hours. Remove the lid, stir and remove the bay leaves. Season with salt. Enjoy over your favorite "healthified" pasta!

TIPS: You can change the flavor profiles to your liking by adding mushrooms, cooked Italian sausage, diced bell peppers, crushed red pepper or whatever you desire. Also, the longer you cook the marinara, the more acidic it will become. Adding fat and/or meat to the sauce will cut the acidic taste. Adding a natural sweetener like Swerve will also help.

HEALTH TIP: About 80% of our sugar consumption is hidden in foods.

NEWMAN'S OWN MARINARA (½ cup): 90 calories, 4.5 g fat, 12 g sugars , 620 mg sodium

Many store bought marinara sauces have over 72 grams of sugar--42 of which don't belong. Sugar is needed when companies use under-ripe tomatoes that are shipped from far away (so the tomatoes don't over ripen in the shipping process). What is more disturbing is the soybean oil in the ingredients.

I make my own in a slow cooker with my own organic tomatoes! But if you must, please buy a marinara with no sugar or soybean oil. Mario Batali has a great product on the shelves now. I found some at Target.

Nutritional Comparison (per serving):

Item	Calories	Fat	Protein	Carbs	Fiber	Effective Carbs
Traditional Marinara	80	3g	4g	10g	2g	8g
"Healthified" Marinara	51	0g	3.2g	5.4g	1.4g	3g

Makes 15 ½ cup servings

Primal Poppers

Ingredients:

10 jalapeños

4 oz. cream cheese

¼ c. sour cream

⅓ c. shredded Parmesan cheese

5 strips bacon, cut in ½

Directions:

1 Slice jalapeños and clean out the seeds (wear gloves if your peppers are extra hot).

2 In a medium sized bowl, mix together cream cheese, Parmesan cheese, sour cream. Stuff the cream cheese mixture into a sliced jalapeño. Wrap half a slice of bacon around the pepper.

3 Lay the stuffed jalapeños in a 4-quart slow cooker. Cover and cook on high for 2-3 hours, or on low for 3-4. Once the bacon is cooked, they are ready to devour. Serve hot or at room temperature.

4 OPTIONAL: Cook and crumble the bacon, set aside. Cut the tops off of the jalapeños, and scrape out the membrane and the seeds (do not cut in ½. In a bowl, mix together your stuffing mixture of cream cheese, Parmesan cheese, sour cream, and crumbled bacon. Fill the jalapeño cavities with the stuffing with a piping bag or a plastic bag with a hole cut in a corner. Put ⅓ cup of water at the bottom the slow cooker, and lay the stuffed jalapeños on top.

Nutritional Comparison (per serving):

Item	Calories	Fat	Protein	Carbs	Fiber	Effective Carbs
Traditional Poppers	219	10g	6g	24.5g	0g	24.5g
"Healthified" Poppers	112	8g	6g	1.7g	0g	1.7g

Makes 10 servings

MSG and Mood

Too many people have this Lipton Onion Soup Mix in their pantry to use for a beef roast or a dip. It seems harmless, just dehydrated onions and spices right? Nope.

INGREDIENTS: Onions (dehydrated), salt, cornstarch, onion powder, sugar, corn syrup, hydrolyzed soy protein, caramel color, partially hydrogenated soybean oil, monosodium glutamate, yeast extract, natural flavors, disodium inosinate, disodium guanylate.

Trans-fat, caramel coloring, soy protein and MSG... yuck, yuck, yuck and yuck!

MSG (an excitotoxin) causes damage to the neurons in your brain and has links to Parkinson's disease, Alzheimer's, Huntington's disease and many others. Children are very susceptible to this type of effect on their sensitive and growing brains. Excitotoxins excite the neurons in the brain too much. They become exhausted and die. Neurotoxins are also a main cause of seizures . The damage may not be seen until many years later. When this happens, our neurotransmitters responsible for focus, mood, and memory have a hard time finding and recognizing their receptors due to the inflammation of the membranes on the brain cells caused by the consumption of MSG.

Brain levels of the neurotransmitter dopamine (important for mood and focus) are lowered by 95% when you ingest excitotoxins. BUT what is even more disturbing, is that when you switch to eating 100% free of processed food, our brain remains unable to produce normal amounts of dopamine in the hippocampus (the part of the brain most responsible for consolidating memory). This is one reason for the high rates of ADHD and depression. To read more on Brain Chemicals, check out my book: Secrets to Controlling Your Weight Cravings and Mood

TBHQ comes from petroleum (think "lighter fluid"). It is banned in other countries. TBHQ keeps fats from going rancid, so you see it in a lot of foods that they want to have a long shelf life. It is considered an "anti-oxidant" BUT it can itself be oxidized into harmful molecules, like tert-butylquinone...causing a TIRED TOXIC LIVER.

Little Smokies recipe is on page 43

Healing Broth

Ingredients:

4 quarts water (reverse osmosis filtered water is best)

Leftover bones and skin from one organic chicken

1 whole clove fresh garlic, peeled & smashed

2 TBS coconut vinegar (or organic apple cider vinegar)

2 onions, diced

2 stalks celery, in ¼ inch slices

1 tsp thyme leaves

Directions:

1   Place the ingredients in a large slow cooker and set the heat to "high." Bring to a boil, then reduce the setting to "low" for a soft simmer. Cook for a minimum of 8 hours and up to 24 hours. The longer it cooks the more nutrients and minerals!

NOTE: mine is a lighter color because I diluted it for my baby boy Kai's bottle. It was too thick to suck through the bottle.

ORGANIC BONE BROTH: stock is so awesome because it supplies hydrophilic colloids to the diet. The proteinaceous gelatin in meat broths has the helpful property of attracting liquids - it is hydrophilic. The same property by which gelatin attracts water to form desserts, like Jello, allows it to attract digestive juices to the surface of cooked food particles. Gelatin acts first and foremost as an aid to digestion and has been used successfully in the treatment of many intestinal disorders, including hyperacidity, colitis and Crohn's disease. Although gelatin is by no means a complete protein, containing only the amino acids arginine and glycine in large amounts, it acts as a protein sparer, allowing the body to fully utilize the complete proteins that are taken in. So these gelatin-rich broths are essential for those who can't tolerate or afford large amounts of meat in their diets. Gelatin also seems to be of use in the treatment of many chronic disorders, including anemia and other diseases of the blood, diabetes, muscular dystrophy and even cancer.

Nutritional Comparison (per serving):

Item	Calories	Fat	Protein	Carbs	Fiber	Effective Carbs
"Healthified" Broth	40	3g	4g	0g	0g	0g

Makes 12 servings

Artichokes

Ingredients:

4 medium artichokes

4 TBS minced fresh garlic, divided

4 TBS balsamic vinegar, divided

1 tsp Celtic sea salt

½ tsp fresh ground pepper

½ c. organic chicken broth

4 tsp butter or coconut oil, melted

Directions:

1   Rinse and cut ½ inch off the top of each artichoke. Trim the stem end so the artichoke can stand flat. Pull the leaves open to stuff with the filling. Mix garlic and vinegar in a small bowl.

2   Spoon 1 tablespoon of the garlic and vinegar evenly between the leaves of each artichoke.

3   Place artichokes in a 4-quart slow cooker. Season with freshly ground pepper to taste. Pour the broth in the slow cooker and add enough water (or more broth) to come up one-fourth the sides of the artichokes.

4   Cover and cook on high 4 hours or until a knife is easily inserted in the stem end and the leaves pull away from the base. Remove from slow cooker and let cool slightly.

5   Drizzle artichokes with 1 teaspoon of the butter, and serve. Makes 4 servings.

Makes 4 cup servings

Nutritional Comparison (per serving):

Item	Calories	Fat	Protein	Carbs	Fiber	Effective Carbs
"Healthified" Artichoke	114	4.2g	5.4g	16g	7g	9g

Chicken Chips

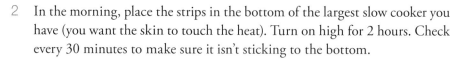

Ingredients:

¼ lb chicken skin (I removed the skin from chicken thighs and saved the thighs for Rosemary Chicken)

1 tsp Celtic sea salt

Directions:

1   Sprinkle the cleaned chicken skin with salt and place in the refrigerator over night, uncovered, to dry a bit.

2   In the morning, place the strips in the bottom of the largest slow cooker you have (you want the skin to touch the heat). Turn on high for 2 hours. Check every 30 minutes to make sure it isn't sticking to the bottom.

3   The "chips" are done when they are a beautiful golden brown and crispy.

Nutritional Comparison (per serving):

Item	Calories	Fat	Protein	Carbs	Fiber	Effective Carbs
Traditional Chips	155	10g	1g	14.1g	1g	13.1g
"Healthified" Chicken Chips	86	7.7g	4g	0g	0g	0g

Makes 6 servings

Green Bean Casserole

Ingredients:

8 c. green beans, cleaned and trimmed

½ c. organic chicken broth

½ c. sharp cheddar, shredded

⅓ c. butter

4 oz. cream cheese

¼ c. onion, diced

Chicken "Chips"

Directions:

1   Place all the ingredients (except chicken chips) in a 4-quart slow cooker.

2   Cook on low for 4 hours or until green beans are soft and the mixture is well combined. Stir every hour to mix the creamy goodness together.

3   Top with Chicken "Chips" (see recipe above).

Nutritional Comparison (per serving):

Item	Calories	Fat	Protein	Carbs	Fiber	Effective Carbs
Traditional Green Bean Casserole	165	12g	3g	15g	1.5g	14.5g
"Healthified" Green Bean Casserole	146	12g	4g	7g	3g	4g

Makes 10 servings

Buffalo Wings

Ingredients:

24 oz. buffalo sauce

2 TBS butter or coconut oil

1 tsp hot sauce

3 lbs. chicken wings (frozen)

⅔ c. "healthified" blue cheese
   (recipe follows)

DRESSING:

2 ½ oz. blue cheese

3 TBS organic beef broth

3 TBS sour cream

2 TBS Organic Mayo

2 tsp white wine vinegar

⅛ tsp garlic powder

Celtic sea salt and pepper to taste

Directions:

1 In a 6-quart slow cooker, combine buffalo sauce, melted butter, and hot pepper sauce. Add chicken wings, stirring to coat with sauce.

2 Cover and cook on low for 3 to 4 hours or until juice of chicken is clear when thickest part is cut to bone (165 degrees F).

3 Serve immediately or keep warm on low heat setting while serving. Serve with "healthified" dressing and celery.

Nutritional Comparison (per serving):

Item	Calories	Fat	Protein	Carbs	Fiber	Effective Carbs
Traditional Wings	279	10g	24.6g	4g	1.4g	2.6g
"Healthified" Wings	193	7.7g	24.6g	2.7g	1.4g	1.3g

DRESSING: In a small bowl, mash blue cheese and broth together with a fork until mixture resembles a broth large-curd cottage cheese. Stir in sour cream, mayonnaise, vinegar, and garlic powder until well blended. Season to taste with salt and pepper. The dressing makes 4 servings.

Nutritional Comparison (per serving):

Item	Calories	Carbs
Traditional Blue Cheese Dressing	241	1.2g
"Healthified" Blue Cheese Dressing	104	1.1g

Makes 16 servings

Sweet Asian Wings

Ingredients:

4 lbs chicken wings

¾ c. Swerve, Confectioners (or equivalent)

1 clove garlic, minced

1 tsp fresh grated ginger

1 c. coconut aminos OR organic Tamari (soy) sauce

¾ c. organic chicken broth

¼ c. lime juice

¼ c. butter or coconut oil

¼ tsp guar gum (thickener)

Directions:

1 In large bowl, mix all ingredients except chicken wings. Add chicken; toss gently to coat.

2 Refrigerate at least 2 hours to marinate.

3 Remove chicken from marinade; place in 4- to 6-quart slow cooker. Add the marinade.

4 Cover and cook on low for 3 to 4 hours or until juice of chicken is clear when thickest part is cut to bone (165 degrees F). Sprinkle with sesame seeds.

OPTION: Make a double batch of marinade. Puree the marinade and serve with the wings for dipping.

Nutritional Comparison (per serving):

Item	Calories	Fat	Protein	Carbs	Fiber	Effective Carbs
Traditional Wings	186	7.5g	22g	7g	0g	7g
"Healthified" Wings	162	7.5g	22g	0.3g	0g	0.3g

Makes 12 servings

Craig's Curry Wings

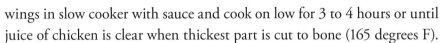

Ingredients:

3 lbs chicken wings

½ tsp Celtic sea salt

SAUCE:

½ c. butter or coconut oil

1 TBS red curry paste

2 TBS lime juice (or juice of 1 lime)

1 TBS Xylitol Honey

1 TBS coconut aminos OR
    organic Tamari (soy) sauce

GARNISH:

¼ c. chopped green onion

Makes 16 servings

Directions:

1 Sprinkle wings with salt. Place wings in slow cooker with sauce and cook on low for 3 to 4 hours or until juice of chicken is clear when thickest part is cut to bone (165 degrees F).

2 Remove from slow cooker and place on serving tray. Garnish with green onion.

Nutritional Comparison (per serving):

Item	Calories	Fat	Protein	Carbs	Fiber	Effective Carbs
Traditional Wings	241	12g	24.7g	4g	0g	4g
"Healthified" Wings	217	12g	24.7g	0.5g	0g	0.5g

Little Smokies

Ingredients:

2 c. tomato sauce

1 c. Swerve, Confectioners
    (or Just Like Brown Sugar)

1 tsp liquid smoke

⅓ c. chopped onion

2 (16-oz.) packages organic mini
    hotdogs

Makes 12 servings

Directions:

1 Stir together tomato sauce, natural sweetener, liquid smoke, onion, and mini hotdogs in the bowl of a 2-quart slow cooker.

2 Cook on low for 2 hours, or until ready to serve.

Nutritional Comparison (per serving):

Item	Calories	Fat	Protein	Carbs	Fiber	Effective Carbs
Traditional Little Smokies	359	22g	8g	28.6g	0g	28.6g
"Healthified" Little Smokies	250	22g	8.5g	3.8g	0.8g	3g

Easy Pizza Dip

Ingredients:

6 oz. ricotta cheese

6 oz. finely shredded Italian
    cheeses

¾ c. pizza sauce
    (no soybean oil or sugar)

Favorite Pizza Topping:
    pepperoni, sausage,
    mushrooms, peppers, onion

Directions:

1   Grease a Little Dipper slow cooker. Spread ricotta cheese in an even layer on the bottom of the crock. Pour pizza sauce over ricotta cheese and spread evenly. Layer shredded cheese over pizza sauce. Layer the top with your favorite pizza toppings.

2   Cook on medium for 2-4 hours or until you are ready to eat "easy pizza." Serve with "healthified" Pizza Hit Breadsticks (see page 44).

Nutritional Comparison (per serving):

Item	Calories	Fat	Protein	Carbs	Fiber	Effective Carbs
Traditional Pizza Dip	149	8g	9g	6g	0.5g	5.5g
"Healthified" Pizza Dip	128	8g	9g	3g	0.5g	2.5g

Makes 6 servings

Pizza Hit Breadsticks

Ingredients:

1 ¼ c. cottage cheese

5 eggs

½ c. coconut flour

1 tsp baking powder

½ tsp Celtic sea salt

PIZZA HUT SPICE MIX:

4 TBS Parmesan cheese

3 TBS garlic powder

1 TBS onion powder

1 TBS oregano

Directions:

1   Line a 4-quart slow cooker with parchment paper and grease well.

2   In a food processor or large bowl, mix the cottage cheese, coconut flour, baking powder, eggs, salt and ½ of the Pizza Hut seasoning until very smooth.

3   Place dough on the greased parchment. Sprinkle with the rest of the spice mix.

4   Turn slow cooker on low for 5-7 hours or until the crust is baked through.

Nutritional Comparison (per serving of CRUST only):

Item	Calories	Fat	Protein	Carbs	Fiber	Effective Carbs
Traditional Breadsticks	304	14g	10g	45g	1.2g	43.8g
"Healthified" Breadsticks	109	4.6g	9.6g	5.2g	2.2g	3g

Makes 9 servings

Italian Meatballs

Ingredients:

1 ½ lbs grass fed ground beef

1 (28-oz.) jar marinara sauce
(no sugar or soybean oil),
divided

1 ¼ tsp Italian seasoning

1 TBS coconut flour

¼ c. chopped fresh parsley

2 cloves garlic, minced

¼ c. onion, chopped

1 tsp Celtic sea salt

1 egg, beaten

Directions:

1   In a bowl, mix the ground beef, ¼ cup marinara sauce, Italian seasoning, coconut flour, parsley, garlic, onion, salt and egg. Shape the mixture into 16 meatballs.

2   Place the meatballs in a 4-quart slow cooker. Cook on low for 6 to 8 hours.

3   Drain any fat from the slow cooker. Add remaining sauce and simmer for 30 minutes.

Makes 6 servings.
NUTRITIONAL COMPARISON:
Traditional Meatballs = 281 calories, 12g fat, 26.2g protein, 12g carbs, 2g fiber (10 effective carbs)
"Healthified" Meatballs = 262 calories, 11g fat, 26.2g protein, 8g carbs, 3g fiber (5 effective carbs)

Nutritional Comparison (per serving):

Item	Calories	Fat	Protein	Carbs	Fiber	Effective Carbs
Traditional Italian Meatballs	281	12g	26.2g	12g	2g	10g
"Healthified" Italian Meatballs	262	11g	26.2g	8g	3g	5g

Makes 6 servings

Mexican Meatballs

Ingredients:

1 lbs grass fed ground beef

½ lb organic ground chicken

1 ¼ tsp cumin seasoning

1 TBS coconut flour

¼ c. chopped fresh cilantro

2 cloves garlic, minced

½ c. onion, chopped

1 egg, beaten

1 (28-oz.) jar salsa

Directions:

1   In a bowl, mix the ground beef, ground chicken, cumin, coconut flour, cilantro, garlic, onion, and egg. Shape the mixture into 16 meatballs.

2   Place the meatballs in a 4-quart slow cooker. Cook on Low for 6 to 8 hours. Drain any fat from the slow cooker.

3   Place the salsa in the slow cooker over the meatballs. Serve with guacamole.

CILANTRO FACTS: Cilantro is one of the richest sources for vitamin K. Vitamin-K plays an important role in bone mass building by promoting osteotrophic activity in the bones. It also has established role in the treatment of Alzheimer's disease patients by limiting neuronal damage in their brain.

Nutritional Comparison (per serving):

Item	Calories	Fat	Protein	Carbs	Fiber	Effective Carbs
Traditional Meatballs	281	12g	26.2g	12g	2g	10g
"Healthified" Meatballs	257	10g	29.4g	8g	3g	5g

Makes 6 servings

Buffalo Meat Balls

Ingredients:

1 lb ground organic chicken

2 oz. cream cheese, softened

2 eggs

2 TBS celery, chopped fine

1 to 3 TBS crumbled blue cheese
(depending on desire of taste)

½ tsp black pepper

SAUCE:

½ c. coconut oil or butter

½ c. hot sauce

RANCH DRESSING:

8 oz. cream cheese

½ c. organic chicken or beef broth

½ tsp dried chives

½ tsp dried parsley

½ tsp dried dill weed

¼ tsp garlic powder

¼ tsp onion powder

⅛ tsp Celtic sea salt

⅛ tsp ground black pepper

Makes 8 servings

Directions:

1 In a medium bowl combine the ground chicken, cream cheese, eggs, celery, blue cheese and pepper. The mixture will be sticky. Form 1 inch balls.

2 Place in a 4-quart slow cooker on medium for 2-3 hours.

3 Once the meatballs are done, add in the butter and hot sauce, stir to coat the meatballs.

4 Leave in slow cooker on very low for your guests to enjoy. Serve with "healthified" Ranch and celery sticks.

Nutritional Comparison (per serving):

Item	Calories	Fat	Protein	Carbs	Fiber	Effective Carbs
Traditional Meatballs	290	22g	19.1g	5g	0g	5g
"Healthified" Meatballs	279	22g	19.1g	0.7g	0g	0.7g

DRESSING: In a blender or a large bowl, mix together the cream cheese, broth, chives, parsley, dill, garlic powder, onion powder, salt and pepper. Cover and refrigerate for 2 hours before serving (it will thicken up as it rests). Makes 12 servings.

Nutritional Comparison (per serving):

Item	Calories	Carbs
Traditional Ranch	153	1.1g
KRAFT Fat Free Ranch	50	11g
"Healthified" Ranch	66	0.75g

Crab Stuffed Avocado

Ingredients:

4 oz. cream cheese, softened

6 oz. canned crab meat
(drained well)

¼ c. tomatoes, chopped

1 TBS chopped scallions, green
part only

¼ tsp Celtic sea salt

¼ tsp pepper

⅛ tsp cayenne pepper

3 large ripe avocados,cut in half,
pits removed

½ c. Parmesan cheese or sharp
cheddar, finely grated

Directions:

1 In a large bowl, combine the cream cheese, crab, tomatoes, scallions, salt, pepper and cayenne; mix until well combined.

2 Cut the avocado in ½ and remove the pit. Fill the avocado with crab mixture, top with generous amounts of cheese.

3 Place avocados on the bottom of an oval 6-quart slow cooker. Cook on low for 2 to 3 hours or until avocado is soft and cheese is melted.

Nutritional Comparison (per serving):

Item	Calories	Fat	Protein	Carbs	Fiber	Effective Carbs
"Healthified" Avocado	290	24g	10.3g	10.3	6.9g	3.4g

Makes 6 servings

Crab Stuffed Mushrooms

Ingredients:

18 medium sized mushrooms, stems removed

3 TBS organic mayonnaise

3 TBS organic sour cream

6 TBS shredded Parmesan cheese

1 tsp finely chopped garlic

1 can (6 ½-oz.) crab meat (or 1 c. fresh crab meat), rinsed and drained well

Dash or two Tabasco

Black pepper to taste

GARNISH:

Green Onions

Directions:

1 Wash the mushroom, remove the stems. Set caps aside on a paper towel to dry.

2 In small bowl, combine mayonnaise, sour cream, Parmesan cheese and garlic. Fold in the crab meat. Add Tabasco and black pepper to taste.

3 Spoon heaping teaspoons full of crab filling in mushroom caps. Arrange mushroom caps (crab side up) in the bottom of a 4-quart slow cooker.

4 Cover and cook on high for about 2 hours. Reduce heat to low and serve the crab-stuffed mushrooms from the slow cooker if desired.

5 Garnish with green onions.

Nutritional Comparison (per serving):

Item	Calories	Fat	Protein	Carbs	Fiber	Effective Carbs
Traditional Mushrooms	76	3.9g	5.3g	5g	0g	5g
"Healthified" Mushrooms	64	3.8g	5.2g	2.8g	0g	2.8g

Makes 9 servings

Greek Mushrooms

Ingredients:

20 large mushrooms

2 TBS butter or coconut oil

½ medium red onion, diced

2 cloves garlic, minced

½ lb ground lamb or sausage

1 tsp Celtic sea salt

½ tsp ground black pepper

½ tsp paprika

¼ c. fresh parsley, chopped

4 oz. feta cheese, crumbled

Directions:

1   Wash the mushrooms, remove the stems. Set caps aside on a paper towel to dry. Finely chop stems.

2   In a skillet over medium heat, add the oil, onion, garlic and mushroom stems. Cook 2-3 minutes until onion begins to soften. Add the lamb or sausage. Season with salt, pepper, and paprika and cook until lightly browned through.

3   Transfer the sausage to a mixing bowl along with the parsley and feta cheese. Stir to combine ingredients and stuff 1 tablespoon of mixture in each cap.

4   Place mushrooms in the slow cooker. Cover. Cook on High for 2 hours.

Nutritional Comparison (per serving):

Item	Calories	Fat	Protein	Carbs	Fiber	Effective Carbs
Traditional Mushrooms	69	3.4g	4.8g	3g	0g	3g
"Healthified" Mushrooms	53	3.3g	4.8g	1.5g	0g	1.5g

Makes 20 servings

Italian Mushrooms

Ingredients:

20 large mushrooms

1 TBS butter or coconut oil

¼ c. onion,diced

2 cloves garlic, minced

½ lb ground sausage

1 tsp Celtic sea salt

½ tsp ground black pepper

¼ c. Parmesan cheese, shredded

2 c. marinara sauce
(no soybean oil or sugar)

Directions:

1 Wash the mushrooms, remove the stems. Set caps aside on a paper towel to dry. Finely chop stems.

2 In a skillet over medium heat, add the oil, onion, garlic and mushroom stems. Cook 2-3 minutes until onion begins to soften. Add the sausage. Season with salt and pepper and cook until lightly browned through.

3 Transfer the sausage to a mixing bowl along with the Parmesan cheese. Stir to combine ingredients and stuff 1 tablespoon of mixture in each cap.

4 Pour the marinara in the slow cooker. Place mushrooms on top of the sauce. Cover and cook on high for 2 hours.

Nutritional Comparison (per serving):

Item	Calories	Fat	Protein	Carbs	Fiber	Effective Carbs
Traditional Mushrooms	88	5g	4g	7g	1g	6g
"Healthified" Mushrooms	77	4.9g	4g	3.5g	1g	2.5g

Makes 20 servings

Bacon Cheese Mushrooms

Ingredients:

16 oz. portobello mushrooms

8 oz. bacon

½ c. onion, minced

1 clove garlic, minced

4 oz. cream cheese

¼ c. grated sharp cheddar cheese

Celtic sea salt and pepper

Directions..

1 Remove mushroom stems from caps and chop stems in small pieces.

2 Chop the bacon in small pieces. In a large sauté pan, over medium heat, cook bacon, onion. garlic and chopped mushroom stems until the bacon is crispy. Reduce heat to low. Add cream cheese and cheddar cheese in the sauté pan and stir until cheeses are melted. Season with salt and pepper.

3 Remove mixture from heat and stuff each mushroom cap generously with mixture.

4 Place the mushrooms in a 4-quart slow cooker on high for 1 hour or on low for 2 hours. Serve warm from slow cooker. Keep on low while your guests enjoy.

Nutritional Comparison (per serving):

Item	Calories	Fat	Protein	Carbs	Fiber	Effective Carbs
Traditional Mushrooms	169	12g	10g	6g	0.5g	5.5g
"Healthified" Mushrooms	156	12g	10g	2.4g	0.5g	1.9g

Makes 12 servings

Artichoke Stuffed Mushrooms

Ingredients:

1 TBS coconut oil

¼ c. onion, chopped

1 clove garlic, minced

24 button mushrooms, stems removed and chopped

1 (12-oz.) jar marinated artichoke hearts, drained and chopped

8 oz. cream cheese, softened

1 c. Asiago or Parmesan, finely shredded

¼ tsp nutmeg

¼ tsp Celtic sea salt and ground black pepper

Directions:

1   Heat the oil in a skillet over medium heat; cook the onions, garlic and mushroom stems in the hot oil until the onion is translucent, about 5 minutes; season with salt and pepper.

2   Transfer the mixture to a large bowl; add the artichoke hearts, cream cheese and Asiago. Season with nutmeg, salt and pepper. Stir the mixture until ingredients are evenly distributed.

3   Stuff the mushroom caps with the mixture. Arrange the stuffed mushrooms in a 4-quart or larger slow cooker.

4   Cook on high for 2 hours and serve warm.

Nutritional Comparison (per serving):

Item	Calories	Fat	Protein	Carbs	Fiber	Effective Carbs
Traditional Mushrooms	145	11g	4g	5.3g	1.3g	5g
"Healthified" Mushrooms	117	9g	5.4g	3.7g	1.3g	2.4g

Makes 12 servings

Spinach Artichoke Dip

Ingredients:

1 (10-oz.) package frozen chopped spinach, thawed and drained

1 (14-oz.) can artichoke hearts, drained and chopped

½ c. cottage cheese

½ c. Parmesan, shredded

½ c. organic mayonnaise

1 c. alfredo sauce

1 tsp garlic powder

Directions:

1 Place all the ingredients in a slow cooker on low heat until melted, stirring occasionally for about 2 hours.

2 Serve with "healthified" bread (use bun recipe from page 118 and one large ball) or low starch veggies.

Nutritional Comparison (per serving):

Item	Calories	Fat	Protein	Carbs	Fiber	Effective Carbs
Traditional Dip	147	8.3g	6g	12g	2.3g	9.7g
"Healthified" Dip	127	6.6g	6.2g	6g	2.3g	3.7g

Makes 12 servings

Crab Dip

Ingredients:

1 lb crab meat (not imitation crab)

3 (8-oz.) pkg mascarpone or cream cheese

½ c. salsa or buffalo hot sauce

1 can chilies and tomatoes, drained

½ c. organic vegetable or chicken broth

OPTIONAL GARNISH:

2 lemons, sliced in wedges

Directions:

1   Cube the cream cheese and put it in a 4-quart slow cooker. Turn on high to begin melting the cream cheese.

2   Add the salsa or hot sauce, milk, and the drained can of chilies. Add in the crab, and stir to combine.

3   Cover and cook on low for 2-3 hours, stirring every 30 minutes.

4   Serve with your favorite "healthified" crackers (recipe in "The Art of Healthy Eating - Kids"), "healthified" bread (recipe on page 118), or celery sticks.

WHAT EXACTLY IS IMITATION CRAB? First of all per serving, it has 15 to 20 grams of carbs! The last I checked crab didn't have any carbohydrates. So where do they come from? It starts with an overly processed white fish (Cod) and fortified with sugar, sugar, and more sugar. Cod is used primarily because it has a mild flavor that easily takes on the flavor of real crab meat, but also because it is cheap.

To create the "crab meat", they mince up the flesh of the fish, and suck out the water to make a thick paste known as surimi. Then they add starch (usually wheat or tapioca) to stiffen up the mixture. It wouldn't be our modern food supply without sugar...so they add that for a preservative so it can last forever in our fridge! Then they add egg whites to stabilize the "crab" which adds gloss and shine. Vegetable oil is also usually added to enhance the texture. If that weren't gross enough... to create the proper color and flavor, manufacturers add a variety of artificial flavorings; such as, carmine, caramel, paprika, and annatto extract – which, also adds the pink color found in real crab meat. Monosodium glutamate (MSG) is also found in some brands to help enhance the flavor. Now is that something you really want to eat? AND do I have to go over what cocktail sauce is made out of??? The first ingredient is usually High Fructose Corn Syrup.

Nutritional Comparison (per serving):

Item	Calories	Fat	Protein	Carbs	Fiber	Effective Carbs
Traditional Crab Dip	205	17.9g	7g	3.9g	0g	3.9g
"Healthified" Crab Dip	177	15g	7g	2.2g	0g	2.2g

Makes 16 servings

Crab Rangoon Dip

Ingredients:

16 oz. cream cheese

4 green onions or scallions, chopped

1 ½ tsp coconut aminos OR organic Tamari (soy) sauce

2 TBS freshly grated ginger

2 TBS Swerve, Confectioners (or equivalent)

½ tsp garlic powder

½ tsp lemon juice

2 c. crab meat (canned is fine)

Directions:

1   Place all the ingredients except the crab in a food processor and blend until smooth. Gently stir in the crab.

2   Grease a Little Dipper slow cooker and place the dip in the slow cooker. Turn on medium and cook for 1-2 hours or until ready to serve.

3   Serve with "healthified" crackers (recipe in "The Art of Healthy Eating - Kids").

Nutritional Comparison (per serving):

Item	Calories	Fat	Protein	Carbs	Fiber	Effective Carbs
Traditional Crab Dip	169	16g	3.8g	9g	0g	9g
"Healthified" Crab Dip	141	13.3g	3.8g	2.2g	0g	2.2g

Makes 12 servings

Stuffing

Ingredients:

"HEALTHIFIED" BREAD

1 ¼ c. blanched almond flour
    (or ½ cup coconut flour)

4 TBS psyllium husk powder
    (no substitutes)

2 tsp baking powder

1 tsp Celtic sea salt

3 egg whites (8 if using coconut flour)

1 c. BOILING water

"HEALTHIFIED" STUFFING:

1 c. butter or coconut oil

2 c. chopped onion

2 c. chopped celery

¼ c. chopped fresh parsley

12 oz. sliced mushrooms

12 c. dry bread cubes

1 tsp poultry seasoning

1 ½ tsp dried sage

1 tsp dried thyme

½ tsp dried marjoram

1 ½ tsp Celtic sea salt

½ tsp ground black pepper

4 ½ c. organic chicken broth, as needed

2 eggs, beaten

Makes 18 servings

Directions:

1   Preheat the oven to 350 degrees F.

2   In a medium sized bowl, combine the almond, psyllium powder (no substitutes: flaxseed meal won't work), baking powder and salt. Add in the egg whites and combine until a thick dough. Add boiling water or marinara in the bowl. Mix until well combined.

3   Form 4 to 5 mini subs (the dough will rise and spread a little) or one large sub/loaf and place onto a greased baking sheet. Bake for 50-65 minutes. Remove from the oven and allow the bread cool completely. Cut in ½ inch cubes for stuffing.

4   Melt butter or coconut oil in a skillet over medium heat. Cook onion, celery, mushroom, and parsley in butter, stirring frequently. Spoon cooked vegetables over bread cubes in a very large mixing bowl. Season with poultry seasoning, sage, thyme, marjoram, and salt and pepper. Pour in enough broth to moisten, and mix in eggs.

5   Transfer mixture to slow cooker, and cover. Cook on High for 45 minutes, then reduce heat to Low, and cook for 4 to 8 hours.

Nutritional Comparison (per serving):

Item	Calories	Fat	Protein	Carbs	Fiber	Effective Carbs
Traditional Stuffing	193	15g	3.4g	17g	1.5g	15.5g
"Healthified" Almond Flour Stuffing	167	14.6g	4.1g	6.1g	2.8g	3.3g

Creamed Spinach

Ingredients:

1 c. organic broth, vegetable, beef or chicken

4 oz. mascarpone or cream cheese

2 TBS butter

¼ c. mozzarella cheese, shredded

¼ c. Parmesan cheese, shredded

½ tsp nutmeg

2 (6-oz.) bags organic baby spinach

Directions:

1   Place the broth, cream cheese, butter, mozzerella, Parmesan and nutmeg in 4-quart slow cooker. Cook on low for 3-4 hours, stirring every hour.

2   Once the mixture is hot and melted, add in two bags of baby spinach. Cover, and set to high for 20-30 minutes, or until spinach is wilted.

3   Stir well to combine and serve.

Nutritional Comparison (per serving):

Item	Calories	Fat	Protein	Carbs	Fiber	Effective Carbs
Traditional Spinach	137	12g	6g	3g	1g	2g
"Healthified" Spinach	90	6.5g	6g	2.3g	1g	1.3g

Makes 12 servings

Sesame Veggies

Ingredients:

SAUCE:

½ c. organic beef broth

2 TBS coconut aminos or organic Tamari (soy) sauce

¼ c. Swerve, Confectioners (or equivalent to taste)

1 tsp guar gum (thickener)

1 tsp lemon extract or 2 TBS fresh lemon juice

1 tsp dark sesame oil

1 TBS fresh grated ginger

1 clove roasted garlic (see page 34)

½ tsp Celtic sea salt

VEGGIES:

2 c. broccoli flowerettes

2 c. cauliflower flowerettes

Optional Garnish:

2 TBS toasted sesame seeds

Makes 4 servings

Directions:

1 In small bowl, combine all sauce ingredients; blend well. Place in a 4-quart slow cooker. Place the broccoli and cauliflower in the slow cooker.

2 Cover and cook on high for 2 hours or on low for 4-5 hours. Season with salt to taste. Top with toasted sesame seeds if desired.

Nutritional Comparison (per serving):

Item	Calories	Fat	Protein	Carbs	Fiber	Effective Carbs
Traditional Sesame Veggies	112	1.6g	3g	23.6g	2.6g	21g
"Healthified" Sesame Veggies	54	1.6g	3g	6.2g	2.6g	3.6g

Alfredo Veggies

Ingredients:

12 oz. fresh broccoli

16 oz. fresh cauliflower

¼ c. cream cheese

½ c. sharp cheddar cheese, shredded

¼ c. Parmesan cheese, shredded

½ c. organic veggie or chicken broth

1 bulb roasted garlic (see page 34)

1 tsp Celtic sea salt

OPTIONAL:

crushed nuts

Makes 8 servings

Directions:

1 Wash and trim vegetables, put in a greased 4-quart slow cooker.

2 Top with the cream cheese, cheeses, and broth. Squeeze the garlic out of the bulb and add it to the mixture. Add salt to taste.

3 Cover and cook on low for 4-5 hours. Top with crushed nuts if desired.

Nutritional Comparison (per serving):

Item	Calories	Fat	Protein	Carbs	Fiber	Effective Carbs
Traditional Veggies	134	10g	5.5g	9g	3g	6g
"Healthified" Veggies	115	7.9g	5.5g	7g	3g	4g

Buttery Mushrooms

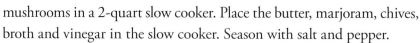

Ingredients:

1 lb mushrooms, quartered

½ c. butter or coconut oil

1 TBS marjoram

1 tsp chives, minced

½ c. organic veggie or chicken broth

2 TBS red wine vinegar

Celtic sea salt and pepper to taste

Makes 8 servings

Directions:

1 Clean and quarter mushrooms. Place mushrooms in a 2-quart slow cooker. Place the butter, marjoram, chives, broth and vinegar in the slow cooker. Season with salt and pepper.

2 Cover and cook for 4 hours on low or until soft.

Nutritional Comparison (per serving):

Item	Calories	Fat	Protein	Carbs	Fiber	Effective Carbs
Traditional Mushrooms	130	11g	2.2g	5g	0.6g	4.4g
"Healthified" Mushrooms	118	11g	2.2g	2.1g	0.6g	1.5g

Creamy "Grits"

Ingredients:

6 c. cauliflower "rice"

½ c. organic vegetable or chicken broth

1 c. mascarpone or cream cheese

1 tsp Celtic sea salt

½ tsp fresh ground black pepper

Makes 8 servings

Directions:

1 Place cauliflower flowerettes in a food processor and pulse until small pieces of "rice."

2 Place all the ingredients in a 4-quart slow cooker and cook on low for 2-3 hours or until the cauliflower is soft.

Nutritional Comparison (per serving):

Item	Calories	Fat	Protein	Carbs	Fiber	Effective Carbs
Traditional Grits	173	4.4g	6g	38g	2g	36g
"Healthified" Grits	75	4.2g	5.3g	5g	1.9g	3.1g

Mashed "Faux"tatoes

Ingredients:

1 head of cauliflower

4 c. organic broth or water

Celtic sea salt and pepper to taste

OPTIONAL:

butter, sour cream, cream cheese,
chives

Directions:

1 Cut up cauliflower into good size pieces. Place in slow cooker. Cover entirely with organic broth or water.

2 Cover and cook on low for 6 hours.

3 Drain water. Use a hand mixer to create smooth and creamy mashed potato-like texture. Add salt and pepper to desired liking.

4 If desired, add butter, cream cheese, sour cream, chives or whatever taste you desire in your 'faux'tatoes. Serve in place of mashed potatoes.

Nutritional Comparison (per serving):

Item	Calories	Fat	Protein	Carbs	Fiber	Effective Carbs
Traditional Mashed Potatoes	129	1.1g	5g	24.4g	3g	21.4g
"Healthified" Mashed "Faux"tatoes	37	1g	4.1g	2.9g	1.1g	1.8g

Makes 6 servings

Creamy Fennel

Ingredients:

2 large fennel bulbs, stalks
removed, halved lengthwise,
and cut in ½" wedges

½ c. heavy cream

1 c. finely grated Parmesan

Celtic sea salt and pepper to taste

Directions:

1 Grease a 4-quart slow cooker. In a bowl, toss together fennel, cream, and 1 cup Parmesan; season with salt and pepper.

2 Cover and cook on low for 4-6 hours or until fennel is tender.

Nutritional Comparison (per serving):

Item	Calories	Fat	Protein	Carbs	Fiber	Effective Carbs
Traditional Creamy Fennel	230	19g	12g	11g	4g	7g
"Healthified" Creamy Fennel	196	12g	11.4g	10g	4g	6g

Makes 4 servings

German "Faux"tato Salad

Ingredients:

1 head cauliflower, cut in small
    cubes

1 onion, chopped

⅓ c. organic broth or water

⅓ c. coconut or cider vinegar

½ tsp guar gum (thickener)

2 TBS Swerve, Granular
    (or equivalent)

1 tsp Celtic sea salt

½ tsp celery seed

¼ tsp pepper

4 slices cooked bacon, crumbled

Directions:

1   Mix cauliflower and onion in slow cooker.

2   In a medium bowl stir the broth, vinegar and guar gum together. Add the remaining ingredients except bacon, in slow cooker.

3   Cover and cook on low setting 6-8 hours or until cauliflower is tender. Stir in bacon.

Nutritional Comparison (per serving):

Item	Calories	Fat	Protein	Carbs	Fiber	Effective Carbs
Traditional German Salad	194	4.4g	4g	34.7g	3.3g	31.4g
"Healthified" German Salad	78	4.4g	3.7g	7g	2.8g	4.2g

Makes 4 servings

Sweet n Sour Eggplant

Ingredients:

2 lb eggplant

2 TBS Celtic sea salt

2 TBS coconut oil

11 garlic cloves, chopped

2 TBS tomato paste (preferably from a tube)

⅓ c. red-wine vinegar

⅓ c. Swerve, Granular (or equivalent)

1 (28-oz.) can whole Italian tomatoes, finely chopped

5 celery ribs, cut in ½-inch pieces

1 large onion, chopped

1 large red or yellow bell pepper, cut in ½-inch pieces

1 c. green olives, pitted and cut in ¼-inch pieces

¼ c. capers, drained and rinsed

½ tsp black pepper

¼ c. chopped fresh flat-leaf parsley

¼ c. chopped fresh basil

Makes 12 servings

Directions:

1   Cut eggplant in ½-inch cubes and transfer to a colander. Toss with 2 tablespoons sea salt. Let drain 1 hour.

2   While eggplant drains, heat 2 TBS oil in a 4- to 5-quart heavy pot over moderately high heat until hot but not smoking, then sauté 8 cloves of garlic, stirring, until golden, about 1 minute. Add tomato paste, red wine vinegar and natural sweetener and boil, stirring, 1 minute. Add tomatoes with their juice, then reduce heat and simmer, uncovered, stirring occasionally, until thickened, 20 to 25 minutes. (Boiling red wine vinegar makes it sweet).

3   Place the mixture in a 4-quart slow cooker and add the rest of the ingredients. Cook on low for 4-8 hours or until you are ready to serve. The longer it cooks, the more the flavors meld. Serve hot or cold.

Nutritional Comparison (per serving):

Item	Calories	Fat	Protein	Carbs	Fiber	Effective Carbs
Traditional Eggplant	93	3.6g	1.4g	14g	2g	12g
"Healthified" Eggplant	62	3.6g	1.4g	7.5g	2g	5.5g

Ham and Cauliflower au Gratin

Ingredients:

1 large head cauliflower (6 c. cauliflower flowerettes, cut in small cubes)

2 c. diced ham

6 oz. cream cheese, softened

¼ c. organic chicken broth

2 TBS finely grated Parmesan cheese

¼ c. green onions

½ tsp Celtic sea salt

Fresh ground black pepper to taste

¾ c. grated Provolone cheese

Directions:

1 Cut the cauliflower in small cubes and place in a greased 4-quart slow cooker. Cut the ham in very small cubes, trimming any visible fat. Add the ham and to the slow cooker. Thinly slice green onions.

2 Stir the cream cheese, broth, Parmesan, sliced green onions, salt and pepper. Stir this mixture into the cauliflower and ham mixture.

3 Cover and cook on medium-low for 4-6 hours or until cauliflower is tender.

4 Remove cover and top with a flavorful cheese such as Provolone.

Nutritional Comparison (per serving):

Item	Calories	Fat	Protein	Carbs	Fiber	Effective Carbs
Traditional Gratin	279	9.7g	7.4g	28g	1.9g	26.1g
"Healthified" Gratin	123	8.8g	7.5g	4.1g	1.6g	2.5g

Makes 6 servings

French Onion Casserole

Ingredients:

3 large sweet onions

1 ½ c. organic beef broth

3 TBS butter

1 tsp coconut aminos OR
    organic Tamari (soy) sauce

1 tsp thyme

½ tsp Celtic sea salt

2 c. shredded Swiss or extra
    sharp cheddar cheese

"HEALTHIFIED" BREAD:

1 ¼ c. blanched almond flour
    (or ½ c. coconut flour)

4 TBS psyllium husk powder
    (no substitutes)

2 tsp baking powder

1 tsp Celtic sea salt

3 egg whites (8 egg whites if
    using coconut flour)

1 c. BOILING water (or
    MARINARA - for more
    Tomato Basil Bread)

Makes 8 servings

Directions:

1   Slice the onions very thin. Place the onions, beef broth, butter, Tamari, thyme and salt in a 4-quart slow cooker. Cover and cook on high for 4 hours or until the onions are brown and caramelized.

2   Meanwhile, make the **"healthified" bread**. Preheat the oven to 350 degrees F. In a medium sized bowl, combine the flour, psyllium powder (no substitutes: flax-seed meal won't work), baking powder and salt. Mix until dry ingredients are well combined. Add the egg whites and mix until a thick dough. Add boiling water or marinara in the bowl. Mix until well combined and dough firms up.

3   Form into a large sub/loaf and place onto a greased baking sheet. Bake for 65 minutes. Remove from the oven and allow the bread cool completely. Slice the bread in 1 inch thick slices (spread butter on each slice if desired). Toast in the oven on a cookie sheet at 375 degrees F for 8-12 minutes or until golden brown.

NOTE: SOME psyllium powder will turn your baked good a "rye bread" color. I have found that Jay Robb psyllium husks (ground into a powder) doesn't cause this to happen. (THIS recipe will make extra bread slices, only use 8 slices, or ⅓ of the loaf for Nutritional Analysis)

4   Once the onions are brown, uncover the slow cooker and top the onions with 1 cup shredded cheese. Top with toasted bread slices. Push the bread slices under the sauce and top with the remaining cheese. Keep the slow cooker on high and cook until cheese is melted, about 20 minutes.

Nutritional Comparison (per serving):

Item	Calories	Fat	Protein	Carbs	Fiber	Effective Carbs
Traditional Casserole	369	20g	10g	46g	2.5g	43.5
"Healthified" Casserole (almond flour bread)	220	15g	11g	10g	3g	7g
"Healthified" Casserole (coconut flour bread)	178	12g	10g	8.5g	2.2g	6.3g

BBQ Shrimp

Ingredients:

2 lbs fresh raw shell-on shrimp

½ c. coconut oil

2 TBS coconut aminos OR
    organic Tamari (soy) sauce

1 TBS Swerve, Granular
    (or equivalent)

1 tsp liquid smoke

1 TBS Tabasco sauce

1 tsp ground black pepper

1 tsp Celtic sea salt

3 lemons, juiced

1 TBS chopped fresh basil

Directions:

1   Rinse the shrimp and place in a 4-quart slow cooker. Add the oil, Tamari sauce, natural sweetener, liquid smoke, tobasco, salt and pepper to the slow cooker. Juice the lemons, and add that, and top with the freshly chopped basil. Mix well.

2   Cover and cook on high for about 2 hours, checking every 30 minutes. You'll know the shrimp is done when it has turned pink, and can be peeled easily.

Nutritional Comparison (per serving):

Item	Calories	Fat	Protein	Carbs	Fiber	Effective Carbs
Traditional Shrimp	177	12.3g	10g	5g	0g	5g
"Healthified" Shrimp	133	10.3g	10g	0.1g	0g	0.1g

Makes 12 servings

Chicken Lettuce Wraps

Ingredients:

4 chicken breasts, ground

5 cloves garlic, chopped

½ c. onion, chopped

¼ c. coconut aminos OR organic
Tamari (soy) sauce

¼ c. organic broth

2 TBS balsamic vinegar

½ tsp fresh ginger, grated

¼ tsp cloves

¼ tsp cinnamon

¼ tsp black pepper

2 heads Boston leaf lettuce or
Romaine

Directions:

1   Grind up chicken or cut in very small pieces. Chop the onions and garlic, dump in slow cooker on top of the meat.

2   In a medium bowl, combine the Tamari, broth, vinegar, ginger and spices. Pour over meat.

3   Cover and cook for 6-8 on low. Serve with Boston or Red leaf lettuce for wrapping.

Nutritional Comparison (per serving):

Item	Calories	Fat	Protein	Carbs	Fiber	Effective Carbs
Traditional Lettuce Wraps	178	5.3g	21.9g	9g	0.5g	8.5g
"Healthified" Lettuce Wraps	150	5.3g	21.9g	2.2g	0.5g	1.7g

Makes 8 servings

Buffalo Lettuce Wraps

Ingredients:

CHICKEN:

4 large (or 24-oz.) chicken breast

2 celery stalk, sliced thin

¼ c. onion, diced

1 clove garlic

16 oz. organic chicken broth

½ c. hot sauce

WRAPS:

1 head of Boston lettuce

2 large celery stalks, sliced

Directions:

1   Place chicken, onions, celery stalk, garlic and broth in a 4-quart slow cooker. Cover and cook on low for 6-8 hours.

2   Remove the chicken from pot, save ½ cup broth and discard the rest. Shred the chicken and return to the slow cooker with the ½ cup broth. Add the hot sauce and set to on low for 30 minutes.

3   To prepare lettuce cups, place ½ cup buffalo chicken in each leaf. Add celery and "healthified" ranch or blue cheese dressing.

Nutritional Comparison (per serving):

Item	Calories	Fat	Protein	Carbs	Fiber	Effective Carbs
Traditional Buffalo Chicken	245	5g	37.5g	5g	0.9g	4.1g
"Healthified" Buffalo Chicken	212	4.4g	37.5g	2.9g	0.9g	2g

Makes 6 servings

Italian Tuna Casserole

Ingredients:

1 head cauliflower, cubed in 1-inch pieces

1 c. diced onion

3 c. alfredo sauce

⅔ c. organic chicken or vegetable broth

2 ½ c. grated cheddar cheese, divided

2 (4-oz.) cans tuna

Celtic sea salt and pepper to taste

1 c. frozen peas (not too many, peas are a starch!)

Makes 10 servings

Directions:

1 Place all the ingredients in a 4-quart slow cooker. Cover and cook on low for 4 hours or until cauliflower is tender. Serve warm.

Nutritional Comparison (per serving):

Item	Calories	Fat	Protein	Carbs	Fiber	Effective Carbs
Traditional Tuna Casserole	400	18g	22.1g	45g	3.1g	41.9
"Healthified" Tuna Casserole	314	22.3g	19.6g	8.7g	1.8g	6.9g

Tuna "Noodle" Casserole

Ingredients:

20 oz. (4 small cans) tuna

2 c. Hearts of Palm, drained and cut in ½ in "noodles"

8 oz. cream cheese

1 c. sharp cheddar, shredded

1 c. organic chicken broth

¼ c. celery, chopped

4 TBS onion, diced

1 pint cherry tomatoes, cut in ½

Celtic sea salt and pepper to taste

Makes 8 servings

Directions:

1 Drain the tuna and the Hearts of Palm. Cut the Hearts of Palm in ½ inch "noodle" shapes.

2 Place all the ingredients in a 2-quart slow cooker on low for 2-4 hours. Season with salt and pepper. Serve warm.

Nutritional Comparison (per serving):

Item	Calories	Fat	Protein	Carbs	Fiber	Effective Carbs
Traditional Tuna Casserole	400	18g	2.1g	45g	3.1g	41.9g
"Healthified" Tuna Casserole	283	18g	24.6g	4.4g	1.4g	3g

Gorgonzola Bisque

Ingredients:

¼ large red onion, diced

½ c. red bell pepper, diced

2 cloves garlic, minced

1 c. organic veggie or chicken broth

1 (14.5-oz.) can diced tomatoes

1 ½ c. tomato sauce

2 tsp dried basil

¼ c. Gorgonzola cheese,
    crumbled

4 oz. cream cheese, softened

¼ c, Swerve, Confectioners
    (or equivalent to taste)

¼ tsp pepper

Directions:

1   Place the onion, pepper, garlic, broth, tomatoes, tomato sauce and basil in a slow cooker on medium for 8 hours or until veggies are soft and flavors meld together.

2   Add the softened cream cheese (you may need to whisk it in to incorporate well). Add the Gorgonzola cheese, natural sweetener to taste, and season with salt and pepper to taste.

3   Cook for an additional 30 minutes for cream cheese to mix with the soup.

Nutritional Comparison (per serving):

Item	Calories	Fat	Protein	Carbs	Fiber	Effective Carbs
Traditional Soup	257	10g	2g	14.3g	2.2g	13.1g
"Healthified" Soup	197	6g	11g	5g	2.5g	2.5g

Makes 4 servings

Cream of Asparagus Soup

Ingredients:

1 ½ lbs fresh asparagus

½ white onion, chopped

2 c. cauliflower, chopped

4 c. vegetable broth

½ tsp Celtic sea salt

½ tsp pepper

4 oz. cream cheese

Directions:

1 Wash and trim the woody ends off of the asparagus. Cut the rest of the asparagus in 2-inch chunks. Place the asparagus in the crock, along with the chopped onion and cauliflower, broth and salt and pepper.

2 Cover and cook on high for 3-5.

3 Add the cream cheese and carefully puree the soup with a hand blender or food processor. Turn slow cooker on low. Return the puree to the crock let the flavors meld until you are ready to serve. Add more salt and pepper to taste.

Nutritional Comparison (per serving):

Item	Calories	Fat	Protein	Carbs	Fiber	Effective Carbs
Traditional Soup	117	4g	5g	14g	2g	12g
"Healthified" Soup	95	5.7g	6g	6.2g	2.6g	3.6g

Makes 8 servings

Cream of Mushroom Soup

Ingredients:

1 lb button mushrooms, cleaned and sliced

1 TBS lemon juice

2 TBS minced shallots

1 tsp dried thyme

½ bay leaf

1 tsp Celtic sea salt

½ tsp fresh ground pepper

4 oz. cream cheese

2 c. organic veggie or chicken broth

Makes 4 servings

Directions:

1 In a food processor, coarsely chop mushrooms in lemon juice. Add all the ingredients to a slow cooker on medium for 4 to 8 hours. You may need to whisk in the cream cheese in to incorporate it well. Add salt and pepper to taste.

Nutritional Comparison (per serving):

Item	Calories	Fat	Protein	Carbs	Fiber	Effective Carbs
Campbell's Soup	166	10g	6.2g	14g	2g	12g
"Healthified" Soup	155	13g	6.4g	5.9g	1.3g	4.6g

Chicken "Noodle" Soup

Ingredients:

4 c. Daikon OR zucchini (cut in noodle shapes)

4 c. chopped, cooked chicken meat

1 c. chopped celery

¼ c. chopped carrots

¼ c. chopped onion

¼ c. butter

12 c. organic chicken broth

½ tsp dried marjoram

3 slices fresh ginger root (optional)

½ tsp ground black pepper

1 bay leaf

1 TBS dried parsley

Directions:

1 Peel and cut daikon with the veggie cutter or by hand to resemble noodles.

2 Place all the ingredients except the "noodles" in a slow cooker on low heat for 6 to 8 hours for the flavors to meld.

3 Add the "noodles" just before serving or they will get too soft.

I used this tool to make my "noodles" ("Spiral Slicer" under "Kitchen Tools"): astore.amazon.com/marisnutran05-20

Nutritional Comparison (per serving):

Item	Calories	Fat	Protein	Carbs	Fiber	Effective Carbs
Traditional Noodle Soup	227	8g	24g	19g	2g	17g
"Healthified" Noodle Soup	120	8g	24g	4g	2g	2g

Makes 10 servings

Smoky Tomatillo Chicken

Ingredients:

2 lbs chicken breast

15 tomatillos, chopped

¼ c. onion, chopped

2 chipotle chiles

4 cloves garlic, minced

¼ c. Swerve, Granular (or equivalent)

1 ½ c. organic chicken broth

2 TBS dried oregano

1 tsp guar gum

Directions:

1 Place the chicken breasts, tomatillos, onion, chiles, garlic, natural sweetener, broth and oregano in a 4-quart slow cooker.

2 Cover and cook on low for 6 to 8 hours.

3 Remove chicken from slow cooker, shred meat using two forks.

4 Remove the sauce from the slow cooker in a medium size sauce pan, sift in guar gum to thicken (make sure to sift in, or it will clump up). Add the shredded chicken to the sauce and stir to combine.

5 Serve over cauliflower "rice" (see page 17) or Miracle rice if desired.

Nutritional Comparison (per serving):

Item	Calories	Fat	Protein	Carbs	Fiber	Effective Carbs
Traditional Smoky Chicken	260	5g	37g	14.7g	1.9g	12.8g
"Healthified" Smoky Chicken	222	5g	37g	5.5g	1.9g	3.6g

Makes 8 servings

Clam Chowder

Ingredients:

¼ c. onion, chopped

1 shallot, sliced thin

1 leek, trimmed, halved lengthwise and sliced

2 celery stalks, diced

4 cloves garlic, minced

1 ½ c. organic veggie or chicken broth

2 TBS butter

2 tsp Celtic sea salt

1 tsp black pepper

1 lb bacon

3 (10oz.) cans baby clams

2 c. clam juice

2 c. cauliflower flowerettes

8 oz. cream cheese, softened

1 tsp thyme

Directions:

1 Clean and chop all vegetables. Place the onion, shallot, leek, celery, garlic, broth, butter, salt and pepper in a 4-quart slow cooker. Cover and let vegetables sweat for 1 hour.

2 While the vegetables are sweating, chop bacon and cook in a fry pan until crispy. Drain excess grease.

3 To slow cooker add cooked bacon, clams, clam juice and cauliflower. Whisk in the cream cheese and thyme. Continue mixing until you can no longer see any clumps of cream cheese and all ingredients are well incorporated.

4 Cover and cook on low for or 6-8 hours.

Nutritional Comparison (per serving):

Item	Calories	Fat	Protein	Carbs	Fiber	Effective Carbs
Traditional Chowder	386	30.1g	24g	9g	0.5g	7.5g
"Healthified" Chowder	319	23g	24g	5g	0.4g	4.6g

Makes 12 servings

Pumpkin Chili

Ingredients:

1 lb grass fed ground beef

1 yellow onion, diced

1 bell pepper (any color), diced

2 cloves garlic, minced

1 (14.5-oz.) can diced tomatoes

2 (4-oz.) cans diced green chiles

1 (15-oz.) can pumpkin

1 c. organic beef broth

1 TBS cinnamon

1 tsp chili powder

Celtic sea salt and pepper to taste

Directions:

1 Add all the ingredients to a slow cooker on low heat and stir well.

2 Cook on low for 7 hours, until meat is cooked through.

3 Serve with "Healthified" cheesey crackers (recipe in "The Art of Healthy Eating - Kids").

Nutritional Comparison (per serving):

Item	Calories	Fat	Protein	Carbs	Fiber	Effective Carbs
Traditional Chili	329	12g	27.4g	32g	4g	28g
"Healthified" Chili	296	8g	27.4g	8g	4g	4g

Makes 6 servings

Lasagna Soup

Ingredients:

1-½ lbs. Italian sausage

2 (32-oz.) jars marinara
    (no sugar or soybean oil)

2 c. organic beef broth

2 pkg Miracle Noodles, fettuccine,
    cut in 1 inch pieces

½ c. fresh basil leaves, finely
    chopped

Celtic sea salt and pepper to taste

CHEESY TOPPING:

8 oz. ricotta cheese

½ c. Parmesan cheese. finely grated

2 c. mozzarella cheese, shredded

Directions:

1   Place the crumbled Italian sausage in a slow cooker on low and let cook for 1 hour or until done. Add 2 jars of marinara sauce and the broth and let simmer for 2-4 hours.

2   When you are ready to eat, add the Miracle Noodles, stir in the basil and season to taste with salt and freshly ground black pepper.

3   While the soup is simmering, prepare the cheesy topping. In a small bowl, combine the ricotta, Parmesan, salt, and pepper.

4   To serve, place a dollop of the cheesy topping in each soup bowl, sprinkle some of the mozzarella on top and ladle the hot soup over the cheese. Serve with homemade "Healthified" Pesto Rolls (recipe in "The Art of Healthy Eating - Savory").

Nutritional Comparison (per serving):

Item	Calories	Fat	Protein	Carbs	Fiber	Effective Carbs
Traditional Lasagna Soup	483	28g	27.8g	26g	1g	25g
"Healthified" Lasagna Soup	373	27g	25.6g	5.6g	1g	4.6g

Makes 8 servings

Provolone "Noodle" Soup

Ingredients:

1 whole chicken, separated thighs, breasts, legs (or 4 large chicken breasts)

4 c. organic chicken broth

1 clove garlic, minced

¼ c. onion, chopped

1 head of cabbage, sliced in very thin noodle shapes

¼ c. cream cheese

1 c. Provolone cheese, shredded

Celtic sea salt and pepper to taste

OPTIONAL:

4 slices of bacon, fried and chopped in small pieces

Directions:

1 In a slow cooker, place the chicken, broth, onion, and garlic on medium heat for 4-6 hours or until the chicken is very tender and done all the way through.

2 Discard the bones if using whole chicken.

3 Add the sliced cabbage "noodles".

4 Turn slow cooker on medium for 2 hours or until the cabbage is soft and noodle texture.

5 Add in the cream cheese and Provolone the last 10 minutes in the slow cooker (the cream cheese may need a little "whisking" to get rid of any small pieces). Season with salt and pepper.

6 Add in bacon pieces if desired.

Nutritional Comparison (per serving):

Item	Calories	Fat	Protein	Carbs	Fiber	Effective Carbs
Traditional Soup	339	11.5g	39g	16g	0.8g	15.2g
"Healthified" Soup	279	10.4g	39g	6.2g	2.3g	3.9g

Makes 8 servings

Cioppino

Ingredients:

1 (28-oz.) can crushed tomatoes with juice

1 (8-oz.) can tomato sauce

¼ c. chopped onion

1 c. organic veggie or chicken broth

2 TBS red wine vinegar

⅓ c. butter or macadamia nut butter

3 cloves garlic, minced

½ c. parsley, chopped

1 green pepper, chopped

Celtic sea salt and pepper to taste

2 tsp basil

1 tsp thyme

1 tsp oregano

½ tsp smoked paprika

½ tsp cayenne pepper

1 deboned and cubed fillet of seabass, cod or other whitefish

12 prawns

12 scallops

12 mussels

12 clams (can use canned)

Makes 12 servings

Directions:

1   Place all ingredients in a 4-quart slow cooker except seafood. Cover and cook 6 to 8 hours on low.

2   About 30 minutes before serving, add seafood. Turn the heat up to high and gently stir. Make sure the seafood is fully cooked after 30 minutes. Serve with "Healthified" bread (recipe on page 118) for dipping in the tasty broth.

Nutritional Comparison (per serving):

Item	Calories	Fat	Protein	Carbs	Fiber	Effective Carbs
Traditional Cioppino	179	6.2g	16g	10g	1.8g	8.2g
"Healthified" Cioppino	163	6.2g	17g	8g	2g	6g

Seafood Bisque

Ingredients:

1 leek, halved lengthwise

¼ c. onion, diced

1 stalk celery, diced

3 sprigs fresh thyme

2 strips orange zest

2 TBS tomato paste

8 oz. cream cheese

3 c. organic chicken broth

1 (12-oz.) bag baby lobster or shrimp, pre-cooked

Celtic sea salt and pepper to taste

finely chopped chives, for garnish

OPTIONAL:

Grilled Brie & Tomato, recipe follows

PROTEIN BREAD:

3 eggs

½ c. unflavored egg white or whey protein

3 oz. cream cheese, room temperature

½ tsp onion powder (optional)

GRILLED BRIE & TOMATO ON CRUSTY BREAD:

1 pint cherry tomatoes

2 TBS extra-virgin olive oil

Celtic sea salt and pepper to taste

3 TBS butter, softened

6 (½-inch thick) slices PROTEIN BREAD

½ lb brie, sliced thin

Makes 6 servings (Bisque)
Makes 6 servings (Grilled Brie)

Directions:

1 Place the leeks, onion, celery, ½ the thyme, ½ the orange zest and the tomato paste in a slow cooker on medium for 2 hours. Whisk the softened cream cheese and the broth together and add to the slow cooker. Season with salt and pepper if needed; keep warm. Open the bag of lobster, drain any liquid and add lobster to the bisque. To serve, ladle the bisque in warmed soup bowls. Top with the Protein Bread Grilled Brie and Tomato, if desired (recipe below).

2 PROTEIN BREAD: Preheat the oven to 375 degrees F. Whip the whites for a few minutes until VERY stiff. Slowly fold in the whey protein and onion powder if using. Then slowly fold in the cream cheese in with the whites (making sure the whites don't fall). Grease a bread pan and fill with "dough." Bake for 40-45 minutes or until golden brown. Let completely cool before cutting or the bread will fall.

3 GRILLED BRIE AND TOMATO: Heat the broiler. Put the cherry tomatoes onto a baking sheet, drizzle them with olive oil, and season them with salt and pepper. Broil them until they burst; set them aside. Butter the protein bread on both sides and top each with several slices of brie. Broil until the cheese is bubbling and slightly browned. Top with the tomatoes. Serve immediately.

Nutritional Comparison (per serving):

Item	Calories	Fat	Protein	Carbs	Fiber	Effective Carbs
Traditional Lobster Bisque	250	16g	18g	13g	1g	12g
"Healthified" Bisque	227	14.4g	18g	6.3g	1g	5.3g

Nutritional Comparison (per grilled cheese):

Item	Calories	Fat	Protein	Carbs	Fiber	Effective Carbs
Traditional Grilled Cheese	306	22g	10.6g	28g	1g	27g
"Healthified" Grilled Cheese	286	26g	14.3g	2.1g	0.6g	1.5g

Fish Chowder

Ingredients:

1 head cauliflower, chopped

½ c. white onion

2 c. organic celery, chopped

1 lb white fish (any fish is fine)

3 c. organic chicken broth

4 cloves garlic, minced

½ tsp freshly ground black pepper

½ tsp Celtic sea salt

2 c. frozen shrimp

4 oz. cream cheese, softened

OPTIONAL GARNISH:

Parmesan Cheese

Directions:

1 Clean and chop up all the vegetables in small cubes. Cut the fish in cubes. Place everything except the cream cheese and the shrimp in a 4-quart slow cooker.

2 Cook on low for 8 hours, or until the veggies are tender.

3 About 30 minutes before serving, stir in the shrimp and cream cheese (you may need to whisk in the cream cheese so it is smooth in the soup).

4 Turn your slow cooker to high for the last 30 minutes.

5 Place in serving bowls and top with freshly grated Parmesan cheese.

Makes 8 servings

Nutritional Comparison (per serving):

Item	Calories	Fat	Protein	Carbs	Fiber	Effective Carbs
Traditional Chowder	159	9g	9.2g	14g	1.3g	12.7g
"Healthified" Chowder	112	6g	9.9g	4.9g	1.5g	3.4g

Cauliflower Soup with Crispy Capers

Ingredients:

¼ c. chopped chives

4 TBS macadamia nut OR olive oil

1 sweet onion, finely diced

3 TBS unsalted butter or
    coconut oil

1 large head of cauliflower,
    chopped in small flowerettes

4 c. vegetable broth

¼ c. capers, patted completely dry

1-2 tsp coconut oil

½ c. unsweetened almond or
    coconut milk

4 oz. goat cheese

Celtic sea salt and pepper to taste

more roasted cauliflower for topping

OPTIONAL:

3-4 TBS macadamia nut oil for
    drizzling on top

Makes 8 servings

Directions:

1   **TO MAKE THE CHIVE OIL:** Place ¼ cup chopped chives and 4 TBS macadamia nut oil in a food processor and blend until smooth. Set aside for garnish.

2   Grease a 6-quart slow cooker. Add onions, butter, chopped cauliflower and vegetable stock, then cover and cook for 2 hours on medium heat or until vegetables are softened.

3   While cauliflower is cooking, fry the capers. Heat a small skillet over medium-high heat and add 1-2 teaspoons of coconut oil. Add dry capers and shake the pan or stir, tossing for 1-2 minutes until crispy and fried. Set aside to drain on a paper towel.

4   Once the cauliflower is soft, place the soup in a food processor with almond milk (make sure it isn't 'vanilla' flavored!), goat cheese and puree until smooth. Add back to the slow cooker. Heat over low heat. Taste and season with salt and pepper. Place in bowls and garnish with crispy capers, roasted cauliflower and a drizzle of oil.

Nutritional Comparison (per serving):

Item	Calories	Fat	Protein	Carbs	Fiber	Effective Carbs
Traditional Soup	225	17g	5g	8.6g	1.6g	7g
"Healthified" Soup	201	16.5g	8.4g	5.5g	2g	3.5g

Broccoli and Brie Soup

Ingredients:

1½ lbs broccoli flowerettes

2 TBS coconut oil or unsalted butter

1 small yellow onion, finely diced

2 ½ c. organic chicken or
    veggie broth

2 c. unsweetened almond milk

8 oz. brie cheese (goat cheese if
    dairy allergy)

Celtic sea salt and pepper to taste

Directions:

1 Grease a 6-quart slow cooker. Place broccoli, oil/butter, onion and broth in the slow cooker on medium for 2 hours or until broccoli is tender.

2 Cut the rind off the brie, and cut the brie in small chunks. Add the brie to the pot.

3 Cover, and cook over the lowest heat for a few minutes to melt the cheese.

4 Place the soup, almond milk (make sure it isn't 'vanilla') in a blender and puree to your desired liking (I left a few chunks in mine). Season with salt and pepper. Serve immediately.

To garnish with a garlic Protein baguette crouton like the one in the picture, preheat the oven to 350 degrees F. Cut 4 ¼-inch slices of Protein bread. Lightly brush both sides of the baguette slices with garlic and butter (or macadamia nut oil) and sprinkle lightly with salt. Bake 15 minutes, until crisp. Float on the hot soup.

Nutritional Comparison (per serving):

Item	Calories	Fat	Protein	Carbs	Fiber	Effective Carbs
Traditional Soup	212	14g	10.5g	10g	2.4g	7.6g
"Healthified" Soup	174	12.3g	10.5g	7g	2.6g	4.4g

Makes 8 servings

Chicken Coconut Kale Soup

Ingredients:

1 ½ lbs skinless, boneless chicken breasts or thighs, cut in bite-size chunks

4 c. kale, chopped

½ c. red bell pepper, seeded & sliced

4 green onions, white and greens part, sliced

3 c. organic chicken broth

1 (14-oz.) can unsweetened coconut milk

2 TBS Swerve, Granular (or equivalent)

2 TBS curry powder

1 tsp dried lemongrass

1 TBS peeled and finely minced fresh ginger

3 TBS fresh lime juice

Directions:

1   Grease a 6-quart slow cooker. Place the raw chicken breast chunks, kale, pepper, green onions, chicken broth, coconut milk, natural sweetener, curry, lemongrass, ginger in the slow cooker and cook for 6 hours on low or until chicken is done.

2   Shred the chicken with 2 forks. Stir in lime juice, serve in soup bowls.

3   **VARIATION:** Add a scoop of cooked cauliflower "rice" (see page 17) to each bowl before you add the soup.

Nutritional Comparison (per serving):

Item	Calories	Fat	Protein	Carbs	Fiber	Effective Carbs
Traditional Soup	309	16.4g	20.6g	22.8g	3g	19.8g
"Healthified" Soup	253	15g	22.6g	8.8g	2.8g	6g

Makes 8 servings

Thai Soup

Ingredients:

4 c. organic vegetable or chicken broth

2 c. coconut milk

1 red bell pepper, sliced in strips

4 oz. sliced mushrooms

2 tomatoes, chopped fine

2 garlic cloves, minced

1 inch fresh ginger, grated

3 TBS fish sauce

½ to 2 tsp red chili paste, to taste

1 tsp Swerve, Granular (or equivalent)

4 limes, divided

½ tsp lime zest

½ lb organic precooked shrimp or extra firm tofu, cubed

Directions:

1 Pour the broth, coconut milk, sliced bell pepper, sliced mushrooms, chopped tomatoes, garlic, chili paste to desired heat, fish sauce and natural sweetener a 6-quart slow cooker. Add the juice of three of the limes, and zest one of them until you get ½ teaspoon to add. Cube the organic tofu (if using) and add the tofu or shrimp to the slow cooker. Stir in carefully, so you don't break up the tofu.

2 Cover and cook on low for 4-5 hours. Garnish with fresh lime slices.

Nutritional Comparison (per serving):

Item	Calories	Fat	Protein	Carbs	Fiber	Effective Carbs
Traditional Soup	169	12g	5g	11g	1.7g	9.3g
"Healthified" Soup	131	10g	5g	5.2g	1.7g	3.5g

Makes 12 servings

Pho Soup

Ingredients:

6 c. organic beef broth

1 lb organic top sirloin
   (flank, sirloin or round)

2 sliced green onions

2 TBS ginger, peeled & grated fine

¾ tsp anise

1 cinnamon stick

1 tsp fish sauce

½ tsp Celtic sea salt

½ tsp black pepper

4 c. Miracle or Kelp Noodles

12 poached eggs

Directions:

1   Pour the broth in a 6-quart slow cooker. Add the meat, green onion, ginger, fish sauce, and spices. Cover and cook on high for 3-4 hours, or on low for 4-6. It's done when the meat is fully cooked.

2   15 minutes before serving, add the entire package of drained and rinsed Miracle noodles to the pot. Push them under the liquid with a wooden spoon, and cover. Serve in bowl and add a poached egg if desired.

3   **POACH EGGS:** Bring 1 in. water to boil in a 12-in.-wide pan. Lower heat so that small bubbles form on the bottom of the pan and break to the surface only occasionally. Crack eggs in water 1 at a time, holding shells close to the water's surface and letting eggs slide out gently. Poach eggs in 2 batches to keep them from crowding, 3 to 4 minutes for soft-cooked. Lift eggs out with a slotted spoon, pat dry with a paper towel.

Nutritional Comparison (per serving):

Item	Calories	Fat	Protein	Carbs	Fiber	Effective Carbs
Traditional Pho	242	6g	19.9g	24g	1g	23g
"Healthified" Pho	146	5.9g	19.9g	2.1g	0g	2.1g

Makes 12 servings

Pork Belly Ramen

Ingredients:

1 lb boneless pork belly

4 c. organic beef broth

½ c. coconut aminos or organic
    Tamari sauce (soy sauce)

½ tsp chili oil (or sesame oil)

½ c. Swerve, Granular (or equivalent)

6 scallions, roughly chopped

1 bulb roasted garlic

2-inch piece ginger, grated fine

1 shallot, split in half

4 c. zucchini "noodles"
    (see page 18) OR
    Miracle Noodles

OPTIONAL:

4 soft boiled eggs, sautéed
    cabbage

Directions:

1 Place the pork belly in a 4-quart slow cooker with broth, Tamari sauce, chili oil, natural sweetener, scallions, roasted garlic (squeeze out the paste from the bulb), ginger, and shallot in a medium saucepan over high heat until boiling.

2 Cover and cook on low for 6-8 hours.

3 When ready to serve, remove pork belly and slice in thin slices.

4 Place pork belly slices in soup broth with zucchini "noodles" or Miracle noodles and other garnishes, like a poached egg and shredded cabbage.

Nutritional Comparison (per serving):

Item	Calories	Fat	Protein	Carbs	Fiber	Effective Carbs
Traditional Ramen	468	35.7g	8g	26.7g	0.5g	26.2g
"Healthified" Ramen	327	32g	6.7g	1.9g	0g	1.9g

Makes 8 servings

Spicy Beef Stew

Ingredients:

1 TBS coconut oil

1 lb grass fed beef stew meat

Celtic sea salt and pepper to taste

2 cloves garlic, minced

1 tsp chopped fresh ginger

1 fresh jalapeño peppers, diced

1 TBS curry powder

1 (14.5-oz.) can diced tomatoes
    with juice

1 onion, sliced and quartered

1 c. organic beef broth

Directions:

1 Heat the oil in a skillet over medium heat, and brown the beef on all sides. Remove from skillet, reserving juices, and season with salt and pepper.

2 Cook and stir the garlic, ginger, and jalapeño in the skillet for 2 minutes, until tender, and season with curry powder. Mix in the diced tomatoes and juice.

3 Place the onion in the bottom of a slow cooker, and layer with the browned beef. Scoop the skillet mixture in the slow cooker, and mix in the beef broth.

4 Cover, and cook 6 to 8 hours on low.

Nutritional Comparison (per serving):

Item	Calories	Fat	Protein	Carbs	Fiber	Effective Carbs
Traditional Stew	393	11g	38g	32.5g	6g	26.5g
"Healthified" Stew	290	11g	38g	8.8g	2.6g	6.2g

Makes 4 servings

Turkey Stew

Ingredients:

BROTH:

1 turkey carcass

9 c. water and 2 TBS granulated chicken bouillon (no msg and gluten) (or 9 c. organic chicken broth)

¼ c. coconut or balsamic vinegar (to extract nutrients)

1 c. onion, diced

1 TBS rosemary

STEW:

2 c. cauliflower, cut in cubes

1 (28-oz.) jar stewed Italian style tomatoes

1 tsp oregano

1 tsp coriander

1 TBS chile powder

4 cloves chopped garlic

Celtic sea salt and pepper to taste

Makes 12 servings

Directions:

1. Place the turkey carcass in a 6-quart slow cooker. Add the water and bouillon (or broth), vinegar, onions and rosemary.

2. Cook on low overnight, or for 12 to 24 hours (the longer you cook it, the more nutrients will be extracted from the bones).

3. Uncover and let cool. When cool, remove all bones from broth, leaving meat inside the pot.

4. Add all the Stew ingredients in the slow cooker with the turkey meat and cook on low for 4-6 hours or until flavors have melded well. Salt and pepper to taste.

ROSEMARY helps extract calcium from the bones of the carcass. "...Voit also found that gelatin improved digestion because of its ability to normalize cases of both hydrochloric acid deficiencies and excesses, and was said to belong in the class of "peptogenic" substances that favor the flow of gastric juices, thus promoting digestion." -Kaayla T. Daniel, PhD, CCN

"Bone broth contains collagen to make your skin supple and radiant. This delicious, mineral-rich broth can be used to make soup to support smooth, strong skin and reduce cellulite." -Donna Gates

Nutritional Comparison (per serving):

Item	Calories	Fat	Protein	Carbs	Fiber	Effective Carbs
Traditional Turkey Stew	328	9.6g	24.2g	32.6g	1.3g	31.3g
"Healthified" Turkey Stew	220	9.4g	22.3g	6.8g	1.3g	5.5g

Creamy Chicken Tomato Soup

Ingredients:

4 (8-oz.) frozen boneless chicken breast

¼ c. onion, minced

2 cloves garlic, minced

2 TBS Italian Seasoning

1 TBS dried basil

1 (14-oz.) can of coconut milk

1 (14-oz.) can diced tomatoes and juice

1 c. organic chicken broth

Celtic sea Salt and pepper to taste

Makes 8 servings

Directions:

1 Place all the ingredients in a 4-quart slow cooker.

2 Cover and cook on low for 9. Remove cover and shred the chicken with two forks. Set the slow cooker on warm until ready to serve.

Nutritional Comparison (per serving):

Item	Calories	Fat	Protein	Carbs	Fiber	Effective Carbs
Traditional Chicken Soup	308	19g	29g	11g	1.5g	9.5g
"Healthified" Chicken Soup	283	16.1g	29g	5.5g	1.5g	4g

Cordon Bleu Soup

Ingredients:

6 c. organic chicken broth

1 lb boneless chicken breast

2 c. ham, diced

2 c. mushrooms, sliced

¼ c. onion, chopped

3 garlic cloves, minced

3 TBS butter or coconut oil

4 oz. cream cheese

½ c. Parmesan cheese, shredded

4 oz. Swiss cheese, shredded

2 tsp tarragon

1 tsp Celtic sea salt

1 tsp pepper

Makes 12 servings

Directions:

1 Place all the ingredients in a 4-quart slow cooker on low.

2 Cover and cook for 6 hours.

Nutritional Comparison (per serving):

Item	Calories	Fat	Protein	Carbs	Fiber	Effective Carbs
Traditional Soup	295	16g	22g	12g	0.5g	11.5g
"Healthified" Soup	245	15.5g	22.5g	3.3g	0.5g	2.8g

Chili

Ingredients:

2 lbs grass fed ground beef

1 lb Italian sausage

2 (28-oz.) diced tomatoes
with juice

1 (6-oz.) tomato paste

1 large yellow onion, chopped

3 stalks celery, chopped

1 green bell pepper chopped

1 red bell pepper chopped

2 green chilies chopped

4 pieces bacon
(fried and chopped)

1 c. organic beef broth

¼ c. chili powder

1 TBS minced garlic

1 TBS dried oregano

2 tsp ground cumin

2 tsp hot pepper sauce

1 tsp dried basil

1 tsp Celtic sea salt

1 tsp ground black pepper

1 tsp cayenne pepper

1 tsp paprika

1 tsp Swerve, Confectioners
(optional)

1 (8-oz.) block Cheddar cheese,
shredded

Makes 12 servings

Directions:

1   Heat a large stock pot over medium-high heat. Crumble the ground beef and sausage in the hot pan, and cook until evenly browned. Drain off excess grease.

2   Place in a 6-quart slow cooker on low. Pour in the diced tomatoes and tomato paste. Add the onion, celery, green and red bell peppers, chili peppers, bacon bits, and beef broth. Season with chili powder, garlic, oregano, cumin, hot pepper sauce, basil, salt, pepper, cayenne, paprika, and natural sweetener.

3   Stir to blend, then cover and cook over low heat for at least 6 hours, stirring occasionally.

4   After 2 hours, taste, and adjust salt, pepper, and chili powder if necessary. The longer the chili simmers, the better it will taste. Remove from heat and serve, or refrigerate, and serve the next day. Top with cheddar cheese and serve with "Healthified" cheesey crackers (recipe in "The Art of Healthy Eating - Kids")!

Nutritional Comparison (per serving):

Item	Calories	Fat	Protein	Carbs	Fiber	Effective Carbs
Traditional Chili	409	21g	23g	28g	6g	22g
"Healthified" Chili	396	20g	31g	12g	4g	8g

Cabbage and Ham Soup

Ingredients:

½ head cabbage

¼ c. onion, chopped

1 green bell pepper, chopped

1 red bell pepper, chopped

1 lb cooked ham, cubed

2 cloves garlic, minced

2 bay leaves

8 c. organic ham or
  chicken broth

Celtic sea salt and pepper to taste

Directions:

1 Slice the cabbage into "noodle" shapes.

2 In a 6-quart slow cooker over a medium heat, place the cabbage 'noodles', onions, bell peppers, ham garlic and bay leaves. Pour the stock over all in slow cooker.

3 Cover and cook for 6-8 hours or until the cabbage is very soft like noodles and the soup flavors have 'melded' together. Season to taste with freshly cracked black pepper, but taste the liquid before adding any salt, as the ham will most likely give off enough saltiness on its own. Remove the bay leaves and serve.

Makes 8 servings

Nutritional Comparison (per serving):

Item	Calories	Fat	Protein	Carbs	Fiber	Effective Carbs
Traditional Soup	334	6.3g	16g	49.3g	3.3g	46g
"Healthified" Soup	154	6.3g	15.3g	8g	3g	5g

African "Nut" Stew

Ingredients:

¼ c. yellow onion, diced

2 green onions, chopped

2 red bell peppers, chopped

4 cloves minced garlic

1 (28-oz.) can of crushed
    tomatoes, with liquid

8 c. vegetable broth

¼ tsp black pepper

¼ tsp chili powder

4 c. cauliflower "rice" (see page
    17) or 2 bags Miracle Rice

1 c. natural sunbutter or
    peanut butter

OPTIONAL:

1 TBS sour cream and a bit of
    tabasco sauce in each serving

Directions:

1   Wash and chop all of the vegetables, and put in the slow cooker. Add the entire can of tomatoes, and the spices. Pour in the vegetable broth.

2   Cover and cook on low for 6 to 8 hours.

3   Add in the cauliflower "rice" (I left my cauliflower in small chunks) and stir in the sunbutter or almond butter. Cook on high for 20-30 minutes, or until fully heated through.

4   For additional "yum" factor, add a dollop of sour cream and a dash of tobasco sauce.

Nutritional Comparison (per serving):

Item	Calories	Fat	Protein	Carbs	Fiber	Effective Carbs
Traditional Stew	255	11.8g	11.6g	25g	4.2g	20.8g
"Healthified" Stew (using Cauliflower Rice)	198	11.8g	11.2g	11g	5g	6g

Makes 12 servings

French Onion Soup

Ingredients:

6 TBS butter

4 large yellow onions, sliced and
separated into rings

1 TBS Swerve, Granular
(or equivalent)

2 cloves garlic, minced

½ c. cooking sherry

7 c. organic beef broth

1 tsp Celtic sea salt

¼ tsp dried thyme

1 bay leaf

12 slices "Healthified" Protein bread

½ c. shredded Gruyère cheese

¼ c. freshly shredded Parmesan
cheese

2 TBS shredded mozzarella cheese

Directions:

1 Heat butter in a large, heavy pot over medium-high heat; cook and stir onions until they become translucent, about 10 minutes. Sprinkle onions with natural sweetener; reduce heat to medium.

2 Cook, stirring constantly, until onions are soft and browned, at least 30 minutes. Stir in garlic and cook until fragrant, about 1 minute. Stir sherry in with onion mixture and scrape bottom of pot to dissolve small bits of browned food from the pot. Transfer onions to the slow cooker and pour in beef broth. Season to taste with sea salt; stir in thyme and bay leaf.

3 Cover and cook on low for 8 to 10 hours.

4 About 10 minutes before serving, set oven rack about 8 inches from the heat source and preheat the oven's broiler. Arrange Protein bread slices on a baking sheet.

5 Broil Protein bread slices until toasted, 1 to 2 minutes per side. Combine Gruyere, Parmesan, and mozzarella cheeses in a bowl, tossing lightly. Fill oven-safe soup crocks ¾ full of onion soup and float a protein bread slice in each bowl. Top with about 2 tablespoons of cheese mixture per serving. Place filled bowls onto a baking sheet and broil until cheese topping is lightly browned and bubbling, about 2 minutes.

Nutritional Comparison (per serving):

Item	Calories	Fat	Protein	Carbs	Fiber	Effective Carbs
Traditional Soup	226	9.5g	9g	24g	1.2g	22.8g
"Healthified" Soup	155	8.9g	11g	5.8g	1g	4.8g

Makes 12 servings

Cheeseburger Soup

Ingredients:

1 lb grass fed ground beef

½ c. white onion, minced

5 c. organic chicken broth

1 cauliflower, cut in 1-inch cubes

2 small garlic cloves, minced

8 oz. cream cheese, softened

16 oz. sharp cheddar, shredded

Crumbled bacon, optional

Makes 12 servings

Directions:

1 Brown the meat on the stove top with the onion, and drain fat.
In a 5-6 quart slow cooker, pour in chicken broth, garlic and cauliflower. Stir in the browned meat and onion.

2 Cover and cook on low for 6 hours, or until onions are translucent and cauliflower is tender.

3 Whisk in cream cheese and cheddar 20-30 minutes before serving. If you'd like the broth thicker, blend a bit with a hand held stick blender. Garnish with crumbled bacon if desired.

Nutritional Comparison (per serving):

Item	Calories	Fat	Protein	Carbs	Fiber	Effective Carbs
Traditional Soup	345	29g	20g	12g	1.6g	10.4g
"Healthified" Soup	305	23g	22g	2.5g	0.6g	1.9g

Cauliflower & Aged White Cheddar Soup

Ingredients:

1 small head cauliflower, cut in flowerettes

½ c. onion, diced

2 cloves garlic, chopped

1 tsp thyme, chopped

3 c. organic vegetable broth

6 oz. aged white cheddar, shredded

2 oz. cream cheese

Celtic sea salt and pepper to taste

Makes 6 servings

Directions:

1 Place all the ingredients in a 4-quart slow cooker. Cover and cook on medium for 3-4 hours.

2 Once the cauliflower is very tender and the flavors have melted, remove from the heat and carefully pour into a blender to puree until smooth.

3 Serve with "healthified" garlic bread (recipe on page 118, sliced and spread with butter and garlic powder), cheese and nuts if desired.

Nutritional Comparison (per serving):

Item	Calories	Fat	Protein	Carbs	Fiber	Effective Carbs
Traditional Soup	269	22g	8.5g	6.3g	1.3g	5g
"Healthified" Soup	146	9g	8.2g	4.4g	1.3g	3.1g

Tomato Basil Parmesan Soup

Ingredients:

2 (14-oz.) cans diced tomatoes,
    with juice

1 c. finely diced celery

½ c. butter or coconut oil

½ c. finely diced onions

1 tsp dried oregano or
    1 TBS fresh oregano

1 TBS dried basil or ¼ c. fresh basil

½ bay leaf

1 c. Parmesan cheese, shredded

4 c. organic chicken broth

8 oz. cream cheese, softened

1 tsp Celtic sea salt

¼ tsp black pepper

Directions:

1   Place the tomatoes, celery, butter, onions, oregano, basil, and bay leaf to a 6-quart slow cooker.

2   Cover and cook on low for 5-7 hours, until flavors are blended and vegetables are soft.

3   About 30 minutes before serving, stir and add the Parmesan cheese, broth, cream cheese, salt and pepper.

4   Cover and cook on low for another 30 minutes or so until ready to serve. Serve with a Parmesan Crisp (recipe follows)

PARMESAN CRISP: Preheat oven to 400 degrees F. Place a sheet of parchment paper onto a cookie sheet. Place a large tablespoon of Parmesan onto parchment lightly pat down. Repeat with additional tablespoons of cheese, spacing the mounds of cheese about a ½ inch apart. Bake for 4 to 5 minutes or until golden. Remove from oven. They will crisp up once cool.

Nutritional Comparison (per serving):

Item	Calories	Fat	Protein	Carbs	Fiber	Effective Carbs
Traditional Soup	268	24g	7g	5.9g	1.1g	4.8g
"Healthified" Soup	198	17.5g	7g	4.6g	1.1g	3.5g

Makes 12 servings

Nutty "Noodles"

Ingredients:

NOODLES:
4 c. cabbage

SAUCE:
4 TBS natural sunbutter or
    peanut butter

4 TBS hot water or organic
    chicken broth

2 TBS coconut aminos OR
    organic tamari (soy) sauce

1 ½ TBS Swerve, Granular
    (or equivalent)

¼ tsp cayenne pepper

1 ½ tsp lemon juice

GARNISH:
Sunflower seeds or peanuts

Directions:

1   Slice the cabbage into thin "noodle" shapes.

2   Place all the ingredients in a 4-quart slow cooker and cook on low for
    4-6 hours or until the cabbage is very soft.

3   You may need to stir the sunbutter into the mixture after 1 hour to
    incorporate well so there are no clumps.

Nutritional Comparison (per serving):

Item	Calories	Fat	Protein	Carbs	Fiber	Effective Carbs
Traditional Noodles	320	11g	5.9g	44.2g	3g	41.2g
"Healthified" Noodles	117	8.2g	5.4g	8g	3g	5g

Makes 4 servings

Swedish Meatballs

Ingredients:

1 ½ lb grass fed ground beef

¼ lb organic pork sausage

1 egg

¼ c. tomato sauce

¼ c. onion, minced

1 TBS coconut aminos OR organic
    Tamari (soy) sauce

1 TBS dry mustard

1 clove garlic, minced

2 tsp Celtic sea salt

1 tsp fresh ground pepper

1 tsp liquid smoke

SAUCE:

1 c. organic beef broth

1 c. cream cheese

¼ tsp guar gum (thickener)

⅛ tsp nutmeg

Directions:

1   In a large bowl, combine the ground beef, pork, egg, tomato sauce, onion, Tamari sauce, mustard, garlic, salt, pepper and liquid smoke. Mix until well combined. Shape into 1.5 inch meatballs and place on baking sheet. Make sure you use a pan with sides.

2   Bake at 325 degrees F 45 to 60 minutes, or until browned.

3   In a medium bowl mix the broth, cream cheese, guar gum and nutmeg together. Place meatballs and sauce in a 4-quart slow cooker.

4   Cook on low for 1-2 hours, until meatballs are cooked through. May be used as main dish served over "healthified" rice (see page 17) or "healthified" noodles (see page 18) or as an appetizer served with toothpicks.

Makes 12 servings

Nutritional Comparison (per serving):

Item	Calories	Fat	Protein	Carbs	Fiber	Effective Carbs
Traditional Meatballs	251	14g	21g	8.9g	0g	8.9g
"Healthified" Meatballs	221	13g	21.8g	1.6g	0g	1.6g

Sloppy Joes

Ingredients:

1 lb grass fed ground beef

2 TBS onion, chopped

1 stalk celery, chopped

1 clove garlic, minced

¼ c. tomato paste (Bionature) in
    a glass jar or tube

¾ c. organic beef broth

1 tsp Swerve, Granular
    (or equivalent to taste)

1 ½ tsp coconut or apple cider
    vinegar

½ tsp mustard

½ tsp Celtic sea salt

⅛ tsp pepper

Directions:

1 Place the beef, onion, celery and garlic in a large greased slow cooker. Turn on low for 2 hours or until beef is done (you want to cook grass fed beef low and slow so it doesn't taste "gamey").

2 Drain the fat. Stir in all remaining ingredients.

3 Keep the slow cooker on the lowest setting so the flavors can meld together (I suggest for at least 4 hours or overnight). Serve on my "healthified" buns (see page 118).

Nutritional Comparison (per serving of meat only: no bun):

Item	Calories	Fat	Protein	Carbs	Fiber	Effective Carbs
With Manwich	298	11g	24.7g	19.3g	1.3g	18g
"Healthified"	228	11g	24.7g	4.2g	1.3g	2.9g

Makes 4 servings

Beef Stroganoff

Ingredients:

1 TBS coconut oil, for frying

1 lb grass fed beef roast

½ c. onion, diced

2 c. mushrooms, sliced

1 clove crushed garlic

4 c. cabbage, sliced into 'noodles'

2 c. organic beef broth

½ c. cream cheese

1 tsp tomato paste

Makes 4 servings

Directions:

1 Heat the oil in a skillet over medium heat, and brown the beef on all sides. Remove from skillet, reserving juices, and season with salt and pepper. Cook and stir the onions, mushrooms, and garlic in the skillet for 2 minutes, until tender.

2 Place the cabbage 'noodles' on the bottom of a 6-quart slow cooker and top with the browned beef. Scoop the skillet mixture in the slow cooker. In a medium bowl, mix the beef broth, cream cheese and tomato paste together until smooth; pour in slow cooker.

3 Cover, and cook 6 to 8 hours on low. Using 2 forks, shred the beef.

Nutritional Comparison (per serving):

Item	Calories	Fat	Protein	Carbs	Fiber	Effective Carbs
Traditional Stroganoff	488	18g	41g	41g	2g	39g
"Healthified" Stroganoff	380	17.5g	41g	8.5g	2.5g	6g

Why Cabbage is Awesome!

1 **HIGH IN VITAMIN C.** An orange is high in vitamin C, but there is also quite a bit of sugar in it. We know that glucose and vitamin C have similar chemical structures, so what happens when we eat sugar with the vitamin c? They compete for one another when entering the cells. And the thing that mediates the entry of glucose into the cells is the same thing that mediates the entry of vitamin C into the cells. If there is more glucose around, there is going to be less vitamin C allowed into the cell. It doesn't take much; a blood sugar value of 120 reduces the phagocytic index by 75%. So when you eat sugar, think of your immune system slowing down to a crawl. Not only is vitamin C essential for immune health, but did you know that vitamin C plays a critical role in preventing osteoporosis by reducing menopausal bone-loss?

2 **WEIGHT LOSS.** It is extremely low in calories and carbs. 1 cup = 39 calories! BUT it also is an excellent weight loss booster for another reason - it contains a chemical called tartaric acid which inhibits the conversion of sugars and other carbohydrates into fat. A simple but effective remedy for weight-loss would be to substitute meals with cabbage salads.

3 **HEART HEALTH.** Cabbage is high in potassium which helps control high blood pressure. It is also high in the amino acid l-glutamine, which plays a very important role in cardiovascular function by supplying a key energy source for endothelial cells that line blood vessels.

4 **CONSTIPATION.** Raw cabbage juice is very effective in curing constipation.

5 **INTESTINAL HEALTH AND ULCERS.** L-glutamine also protects the stomach lining. Drinking a lot of cabbage juice daily can also help heal ulcers. I often recommend my clients to take the supplement l-glutamine, but eating cabbage can also help heal the stomach, intestines (IBS, crohn's, colitis), and colon.

6 **IT IS CHEAP AND IT LASTS A LONG TIME IN THE FRIDGE!** I always keep one in the fridge.

French Dip Sandwiches

Ingredients:

1 (4 lb) boneless grass fed beef roast

⅓ c. coconut aminos OR organic
    Tamari (soy) sauce

1 bay leaf

3 whole black peppercorns

1 tsp dried rosemary, crushed

½ tsp dried thyme

1 tsp garlic powder

4 c. organic beef broth

8 "Healthified" Buns
    (see page 118)

OPTIONAL:

16 slices Provolone cheese

butter for rolls

Directions:

1 Remove and discard all visible fat from the roast. Place trimmed roast in a 4-quart slow cooker.

2 In a medium bowl, combine Tamari sauce, bay leaf, peppercorns, rosemary, thyme, and garlic powder. Pour mixture over roast. Add the beef broth to the slow cooker.

3 Cover, and cook on Low heat for 6-8 hours, or until meat is very tender.

4 Preheat oven to 350 degrees for toasting the rolls. Remove meat from broth, reserving broth. Slice or shred meat depending on your preference.

5 Slice the "healthified" rolls in half and place on a cooking sheet. Spread with butter and bake in the oven for 2-3 minutes or until barely toasted. Place meat on rolls and top each roll with 2 slices of Provolone cheese. Put rolls back in the oven for 2-3 minutes or until cheese is melted. Skim fat off the surface of the reserved broth in the slow cooker. Serve with reserved broth in ramekins for dipping sandwiches.

Nutritional Comparison (per serving):

Item	Calories	Fat	Protein	Carbs	Fiber	Effective Carbs
Traditional French Dip	223	7g	35.2g	1.3g	0g	1.3g
"Healthified" French Dip	218	7g	35.2	0.3g	0g	0.3g

Makes 8 servings

Philly Cheesesteak

Ingredients:

2 lb. grass fed beef strip loin

1 sliced onion

2 orange pepper, sliced

1 red pepper, sliced

2 c. organic beef broth

¼ c. coconut aminos OR organic
    Tamari (soy) sauce

garlic, Celtic sea salt and pepper
    if desired

Directions:

1   Place beef, onion and peppers in the bottom of the slow cooker. Pour broth and soy sauce over the beef.

2   Cook on low for 8-9 hours, or on high for 4-6 hours.

3   When done, you can place the mixture onto "Healthified" Buns (see page 118) and top with cheese (mozzarella or Provolone). But it tastes great without bread too!

Nutritional Comparison (per serving):

Item	Calories	Fat	Protein	Carbs	Fiber	Effective Carbs
Traditional Philly	571	19g	53g	48g	6g	42g
"Healthified" Philly (without Protein Bun)	351	17g	43g	4.2g	1.1g	3.1g
"Healthified" Philly (with Protein Bun)	397	20g	65g	4.8g	1.1g	3.7g

Makes 8 servings

Blue Cheese Steak Roll-Ups

Ingredients:

1 ½ lbs grass fed beef (round tip)

½ c. organic beef broth

¼ c. coconut aminos OR organic
   Tamari (soy) sauce

1 TBS Swerve, Granular
   (or equivalent)

4 cloves garlic

6 oz. blue cheese

Directions:

1 Flatten the beef by placing it in a Ziplock bag and pounding it with a
   mallet until it is ½ inch thick.

2 In a medium bowl, combine the broth, Tamari sauce, natural sweetener
   and garlic. Place the meat in the bowl, cover and refrigerate overnight
   or for 8 hours.

3 One at a time, take the meat out of the marinade mixture, lay it flat
   and place the cheese all over one side. Roll it up and secure it shut
   with toothpicks.

4 Place in a 4-quart slow cooker, and repeat with the remaining slabs of
   meat. Cover and cook on low for 3 to 4 hours. Remove the toothpicks
   and enjoy.

Nutritional Comparison (per serving):

Item	Calories	Fat	Protein	Carbs	Fiber	Effective Carbs
Traditional Steak	333	15.3g	41g	5.6g	0g	5.6g
"Healthified" Steak	317	15.3g	41g	1.4g	0g	1.4g

Makes 6 servings

Beefy "Noodles"

Ingredients:

4 lbs grass fed chuck roast

1 clove garlic, mashed

Celtic sea salt and pepper to taste

1 rib celery, chopped

½ c. onion, sliced

4 c. mushrooms, sliced

¾ c. sour cream or cream cheese

¼ tsp guar gum (thickener)

NOODLES:

½ head cabbage

1 c. organic beef broth

Directions:

1   Rub roast with garlic and season with salt and pepper. Place the roast in a 4-quart slow cooker and top with celery, onion and mushrooms.

2   Cover and cook on low 8 to 10 hours.

3   About 30 minutes before serving, whisk the sour cream and guar gum together and add it to the slow cooker. Serve with hot cabbage noodles. Add in additional sour cream if you desire.

4   To make the cabbage noodles, slice the cabbage into thin "noodle-like" shapes. Place in a separate 6-quart slow cooker and cover with about 1 cup organic beef broth. Cook on low for 6 to 8 hours or until soft "noodles." Drain and set aside for the beef.

Nutritional Comparison (per serving):

Item	Calories	Fat	Protein	Carbs	Fiber	Effective Carbs
Traditional Beefy Noodles	469	19.3g	41g	25.3g	0g	25.3g
"Healthified" Beefy Noodles	352	18g	41g	3.6g	1.1g	2.5g

Makes 12 servings

Goat Cheese Meatloaf

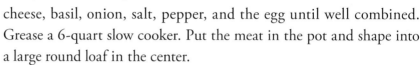

Ingredients:

1 lb grass fed ground beef

4 oz. goat cheese crumbles

4 TBS fresh basil, chopped
(or 1 TBS dried basil)

1 TBS onion, minced

1 tsp Celtic sea salt

½ tsp black pepper

1 egg

Directions:

1 In a large mixing bowl, mix the meat, cheese, basil, onion, salt, pepper, and the egg until well combined. Grease a 6-quart slow cooker. Put the meat in the pot and shape into a large round loaf in the center.

2 Cover and cook on low for 7-8. The meat is done when it is cooked thoroughly and has browned on top and darkened on the edges.

3 Lift the meat out of the crock and let it stand on a cutting board for 15 minutes before cutting.

Nutritional Comparison (per serving):

Item	Calories	Fat	Protein	Carbs	Fiber	Effective Carbs
Traditional Meatloaf	328	17.7g	27.9g	6g	0g	6g
"Healthified" Meatloaf	307	17g	27.9g	1.6g	0.8g	0.8g

Makes 4 servings

Meatloaf "Cup"cake

Directions:

1 Use the meatloaf recipe from page 104 or meatball recipe from page 45. Place mixture in a cute tea cup. Place the cups in the largest slow cooker you own. Fill the slow cooker with water to surround the cups (making sure no water gets in the cups with the meat). Cook on low for 8 hours or until meat is cooked through.

2 Carefully remove the cups from the slow cooker. Top with "faux"tatoes (see page 61) and a cherry tomato!

Easy Ribs

Ingredients:

4 lbs pork baby back ribs

⅓ c. Swerve, Confectioners (or equivalent)

1 TBS paprika

1 ½ tsp chili powder

1 ½ tsp Celtic sea salt

1 tsp ground cumin

1 tsp fresh ground pepper

¾ tsp ground oregano

½ tsp cayenne pepper

¼ c. tomato sauce

Makes 16 servings

Directions:

1   Trim excess fat from ribs. Combine dry ingredients and rub over the surface of the ribs.

2   Place ribs in a 4-quart slow cooker standing on their edge with the meaty side out. Add the tomato sauce. Cover and cook on low for 7-8 hours.

Nutritional Comparison (per serving):

Item	Calories	Fat	Protein	Carbs	Fiber	Effective Carbs
Traditional Ribs	429	31g	25g	12g	0g	12g
"Healthified" Ribs	394	31g	25g	0.8g	0g	0.8g

Smoky Baby Back Ribs

Ingredients:

2 lbs baby back pork ribs

¼-½ tsp smoked paprika

GLAZE:

4 TBS tomato sauce

2 TBS xylitol

1 tsp liquid smoke

NOTE: xylitol melts nicely where erythritol doesn't melt

Directions:

1   Spray inside of crock with coconut oil spray. Cut ribs with scissors in 3- or 4-rib chunks and place in crock. Sprinkle with smoked paprika.

2   Cook on low for 8-10 hours. Test with a fork to make sure they are tender. Meanwhile, mix the glaze ingredients and set aside.

3   When ready to serve, remove ribs from crock, place them on a foil- or parchment paper-lined baking sheet, brush ribs with glaze and broil or grill ribs to get a crispy outside.

Nutritional Comparison (per serving):

Item	Calories	Fat	Protein	Carbs	Fiber	Effective Carbs
Traditional Ribs	692	54g	36g	12g	0g	12g
"Healthified" Ribs	640	54g	36g	0.9g	0g	0.9g

Makes 4 servings

Pepper Venison Steak

Ingredients:

2 lbs venison sirloin, cut in 2-inch strips

2 cloves garlic, roasted and smashed

3 TBS coconut oil

½ c. organic beef broth

½ tsp guar gum (thickener)

½ c. chopped onion

1 red bell pepper, sliced

1 green bell peppers, sliced

1 (14.5-oz.) jar stewed tomatoes, with liquid

3 TBS coconut aminos OR organic Tamari (soy) sauce

1 TBS Swerve, Granular (or equivalent)

1 tsp Celtic sea salt

Directions:

1   Rub strips of sirloin with smashed garlic. In a large skillet over medium heat, heat the oil and brown the seasoned beef strips. Transfer to a slow cooker.

2   Mix the broth and guar gum until smooth. Pour in the slow cooker with meat. Stir in onion, green peppers, stewed tomatoes, Tamari sauce, natural sweetener, and salt.

3   Cover, and cook on low for 6 to 7 hours.

Nutritional Comparison (per serving):

Item	Calories	Fat	Protein	Carbs	Fiber	Effective Carbs
Traditional Venison Steak	268	8g	35.1g	9.9g	1.4g	8.5g
"Healthified" Venison Steak	238	8g	35.1g	4.8g	1.4g	3.4g

Makes 8 servings

Paprika Tenderloin

Ingredients:

2 lb pork or venison tenderloin

1 TBS coconut flour

4 TBS smoky paprika

½ tsp Celtic sea salt

¼ tsp fresh ground pepper

1 TBS coconut oil

½ c. onion, sliced

½ c. organic chicken broth

½ c. organic crème fraîche or
    sour cream

Directions:

1   Wash and pat the meat dry. Combine coconut flour, paprika, salt, and pepper in a food storage bag. Toss the meat in the bag and coat thoroughly.

2   Heat the oil in a large skillet over medium-high heat. Add the pork and onions; brown for about 5 to 6 minutes, turning pork ribs once to brown both sides. Place the meat and onions in a 4-quart slow cooker. Pour chicken broth in the hot pan and scrape up browned bits; pour in the slow cooker. Cover and cook on LOW for 6 to 8 hours or until fork tender. Remove meat and place onto a tray.

3   Pour juices in a saucepan and place over medium heat. Simmer for 5 to 8 minutes, until reduced by about ¼ to ⅓. Remove from heat and stir in sour cream; serve the sauce with the loin.

Nutritional Comparison (per serving):

Item	Calories	Fat	Protein	Carbs	Fiber	Effective Carbs
Traditional Tenderloin	233	9g	30g	6.4g	0g	6.4g
"Healthified" Tenderloin	221	9g	30.8g	2.4g	0.8g	1.6g

Makes 8 servings

Shredded Beef

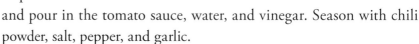

Ingredients:

BEEF

1 (4 lb) grass fed beef chuck roast

1 c. tomato sauce

½ c. water or organic beef broth

½ c. coconut or red wine vinegar

1 TBS chili powder

Celtic sea salt and pepper to taste

2 garlic cloves, minced

"FAUX"TATOES

See page 61

Makes 12 servings

Directions:

1   Place the roast a 4-quart slow cooker and pour in the tomato sauce, water, and vinegar. Season with chili powder, salt, pepper, and garlic.

2   Cook on low heat for 6 to 8 hours, or until meat is fork tender.

3   Shred beef. Serve alone, or over the "faux"tatoes.

4   Top with white cheddar cheese and a cherry!

Nutritional Comparison (per serving, with ¼ pound hot beef):

Item	Calories	Fat	Protein	Carbs	Fiber	Effective Carbs
Traditional Beef Sundae	701	41g	39g	40.7g	1g	39.7g
"Healthified" Beef Sundae	535	28g	38g	9g	3.8g	5.2g

"Smoked" Beef Brisket

Ingredients:

4 lbs grass fed beef brisket, or chuck roast

2 tsp celery salt

½ TBS garlic powder

½ tsp freshly ground pepper

½ c. tomato sauce

½ c. liquid smoke

Makes 12 servings

Directions:

1   Place the meat in a 4-quart slow cooker, add spices to coat the meat. Stir in tomato sauce and liquid smoke. Cover and cook on low for 8-10 hours.

2   Serve with healthified "corn" bread (see "The Art of Healthy Eating - Savory").

Nutritional Comparison (per serving):

Item	Calories	Fat	Protein	Carbs	Fiber	Effective Carbs
Traditional Brisket	435	28.3g	38.3g	5g	2.7g	2.3g
"Healthified" Brisket	331	12.6g	50.1g	0.9g	0g	0.9g

Stuffed Tenderloin

Ingredients:

2 lb venison or pork tenderloin

½ c. gorgonzola cheese

½ c. feta cheese

2 cloves minced garlic

2 tbs finely crushed almonds

1 tsp finely chopped onion

½ tsp Celtic sea salt

½ tsp freshly ground pepper

Directions:

1 Make pocket in tenderloin. In a medium mix bowl mix the Gorgonzola, feta, garlic, almonds and onions. Stuff the cheese mixture into the pocket. Seal the meat shut with skewer. Salt and pepper the meat. Completely wrap the loin in foil.

2 Cover and cook on low for 6 hours.

Makes 8 servings

Nutritional Comparison (per serving):

Item	Calories	Fat	Protein	Carbs	Fiber	Effective Carbs
Traditional Stuffed Loin	194	6.2g	28.8g	2.9g	0g	2.9g
"Healthified" Stuffed Loin	194	6.9g	29g	1.7g	0g	1.7g

Perfect Pulled Pork

Ingredients:

3.5 lbs boneless pork shoulder roast

5 cloves fresh garlic, sliced

2 TBS paprika

1 tsp garlic powder

1 tsp chili powder

1 tsp Celtic sea salt

1 tsp freshly grated pepper

1 medium yellow onion

2 tsp liquid smoke

3 c. organic chicken broth or water

Directions:

1   Using a sharp paring knife, cut deep slits in the meat and push slices of garlic inside the slits. Mix the paprika, garlic powder, chili powder, salt and fresh black pepper in a bowl for a rub. Place the seasoned roast in a ziplock bag or in a dish that you can cover tightly. Dice the onion and add to the bag or dish. Then add the liquid smoke. Let the roast sit in the refrigerator over night to absorb the spices.

2   Place the contents of the bag in a 4-quart slow cooker. Add in 3 cups broth or water. Cover and cook on low for 8 hours (test with a meat thermometer to make sure it reads 160 degrees F). Using a fork, shred the pork. Use for sandwiches on "healthified" buns (see page 118).

Nutritional Comparison (per serving):

Item	Calories	Fat	Protein	Carbs	Fiber	Effective Carbs
Traditional Pork Sandwich	231	4.8g	35g	10.4g	0.7g	9.7g
"Healthified" Pork Sandwich	199	4.8g	35g	2.1g	0.7g	1.4g

Makes 12 servings

Pot Roast Pork

Ingredients:

4 lbs boneless pork or venison
   loin roast, trimmed

8 cloves garlic, slivered

½ c. onion, sliced

2 bay leaves

3 TBS coconut aminos OR
   organic Tamari (soy) sauce

½ c. water or organic broth

½ tsp Celtic sea salt

½ tsp freshly grated pepper

¼ tsp guar gum (if desired)

Directions:

1   Rub the pork roast with salt and pepper. Make tiny slits in meat and insert slivers of garlic. Put the sliced onion in bottom of a 4-quart slow cooker, place prepared roast on top, add the remaining ingredients except guar gum.

2   Cover and cook on low for 6 to 8 hours (test with a meat thermometer to make sure it reads 160 degrees F).

3   Remove roast to a platter. Slice and serve. Thicken juices with ¼ to ½ tsp guar gum to use as gravy if desired.

Nutritional Comparison (per serving):

Item	Calories	Fat	Protein	Carbs	Fiber	Effective Carbs
Traditional Pork Roast	290	12g	38g	3.9g	0g	3.9g
"Healthified" Pork Roast	274	12g	38g	0.7g	0g	0.7g

Makes 14 servings

Parmesan Honey Pork

Ingredients:

2 lbs boneless pork roast

⅔ c. Parmesan cheese, grated

½ c. Xylitol honey
   (no substitutes)

½ c. tomato sauce

1 TBS dried basil

2 TBS coconut oil or butter

½ tsp Celtic sea salt

"FAUX"TATOES
See page 61

Directions:

1   Grease a 4-quart slow cooker. Place roast in the slow cooker. In a small bowl, combine the cheese, xylitol honey, tomato sauce, basil, oil and salt; pour over pork. Cover and cook on low for 6-7 hours or until a meat thermometer reads 160 degrees F.

2   Remove meat to a serving platter; keep warm. Skim fat from cooking juices; transfer to a small saucepan. Bring liquid to a boil and cook and stir for 2 minutes or until thickened. Slice or shred the roast; serve with sauce and mashed "faux"tatoes.

NOTE: The only thing changed in the Nutritional Comparison was using real honey. For anyone with a damaged metabolism or metabolic syndrome (or wanting to lose weight) even that small amount of honey in each serving will be detrimental. The honey bear is the only animal found in nature with a problem with tooth-decay (honey decays teeth faster than table sugar). Honey = highest calorie content of all sugars with 65 calories/TBS, compared to the 48 calories/TBS found in table sugar.

Nutritional Comparison (per serving):

Item	Calories	Fat	Protein	Carbs	Fiber	Effective Carbs
Traditional Honey Pork	296	9.8g	33g	18.6g	0g	18.6g
"Healthified" Honey Pork	231	9.8g	33g	1.2g	0g	1.2g

Makes 12 servings

Pork Lettuce Cups

Ingredients:

1 lb ground pork

½ c. onion, chopped

2 cloves fresh garlic, minced

1 TBS coconut aminos OR organic
   Tamari (soy) sauce

2 tsp minced ginger

1 TBS coconut or rice wine vinegar

1 bunch green onions, chopped

2 tsp Asian (dark) sesame oil

SAUCE:

½ c. fresh lime juice

2 TBS fish sauce

3 TBS Swerve, Confectioners
   (or equivalent)

Celtic sea salt to taste

1 tsp Asian chile sauce, such as sambal oelek

1 clove garlic, minced

1 tsp ginger, minced

FIXINGS:

1 head Boston lettuce, leaves separated

½ bunch mint

½ bunch basil

½ bunch cilantro

1 English cucumber, thinly sliced

1 red jalapeño pepper, seeded and sliced

1 c. prepared fried scallions or onions

Makes 4 servings

Directions:

1   Place the pork, garlic, Tamari sauce, ginger, vinegar, green onions, and sesame oil in a greased 4-quart slow cooker. Cover and cook on low for 4 hours or until pork is done. Meanwhile, prepare the dipping sauce by mixing all the ingredients in a cute dish. Set aside until ready to serve.

2   Rinse whole lettuce leaves and pat dry, being careful not tear them. Arrange lettuce leaves around the outer edge of a large serving platter, and pile meat mixture in the center. To serve, allow each person to spoon a portion of the meat in a lettuce leaf and fill with desired herbs. Wrap the lettuce around the meat like a burrito, and enjoy!

What is coconut vinegar you may ask when you see this recipe. Well, Coconut vinegar exceeds all other vinegars in amino acids, vitamins and mineral content. Don't worry, it doesn't taste like coconut! Here are some reasons why I love it!

1. It is also a FOS (a prebiotic that promotes digestive health).

2. The sap used to make coconut vinegar comes from coconut trees grown in volcanic soil rich with minerals. No need to worry about your potassium if you don't eat potatoes or bananas (because they are too high in sugar/starch), coconut vinegar has 192mg per tablespoon!!! The sap also contains large amounts of phosphorus, potassium, iron, magnesium, sulfur, boron, zinc, manganese and copper.

3. Coconut sap has all 9 essential amino acids, which are the building blocks of protein. It also contains 8 nonessential amino acids. Proteins are part of every living cell in your body, it forms hemoglobin, which carries oxygen and antibodies, which boosts the immune system. Amino acids also repair tissue, serve as neurotransmitters, transmits messages within the brain, and some detoxify your body and boost metabolic functions.

4. It is low on the glycemic index, coming in at only 35 on the scale.

This natural vinegar is a great replacement for your recipes that call for other vinegars. I use it for Kai's bone broth, soups, dips, salad dressings, marinades...you name it.

Nutritional Comparison (per serving):

Item	Calories	Fat	Protein	Carbs	Fiber	Effective Carbs
Traditional Pork Cups	388	22g	23g	25g	4g	21g
"Healthified" Pork Cups	223	4.7g	32g	8g	2.5g	5.5g

Pork Cabbage Rolls

Ingredients:

1 large head green cabbage

2 TBS coconut oil

1 c. finely chopped onions

¼ tsp of finely chopped garlic

1 lb ground lean pork

2 lightly beaten eggs

1 tsp Celtic sea salt

½ tsp freshly ground pepper

2 TBS sweet paprika

¼ tsp marjoram

2 lbs sauerkraut

2 c. tomato sauce

OPTIONAL:

1 c. sour cream

Directions:

1 In a large saucepan, bring to a boil enough salted water to cover the cabbage. Add the cabbage, turn the heat to low and simmer 8 minutes. Remove the cabbage and let it drain while it cools enough to handle. Pull off 16 large cabbage leaves and lay them on paper towels to drain.

2 In a large skillet, sauté the onions and garlic in coconut oil, until the onions are lightly colored. In a large mixing bowl, combine the pork, eggs, the onion-garlic mixture, salt, pepper and spices. Place 2 tablespoons of this mixture in the center of one of the soft cabbage leaves and, beginning with the thick end of the leaf, fold over the sides, then roll the whole leaf tightly, as you would a small bundle. Repeat until all the stuffing has been used.

3 Drain the sauerkraut and spread on the bottom of a 6-quart slow cooker and arrange the cabbage rolls on top of it. Add the tomato sauce. Cook on low for 2 hours or until you are ready to serve. Stir in the sour cream (if using) to the sauerkraut. Heat for another 10 minutes. Lift the sauerkraut onto a serving platter with a slotted spoon. Arrange the cabbage rolls on the sauerkraut and pour the sauce over the rolls and serve.

Nutritional Comparison (per serving):

Item	Calories	Fat	Protein	Carbs	Fiber	Effective Carbs
Cabbage Rolls	279	18g	18g	14g	7g	7g

Makes 6 servings

Sausage and Veggies

Ingredients:

4 c. mushrooms

1 c. broccoli flowerettes

1 c. cauliflower flowerettes

1 red bell pepper

6 organic chicken sausage links, cut into ¼-inch pieces

1 c. organic chicken broth

Makes 6 servings

Directions:

1 Cut all veggies into 2-inch chunks. Place in a 2-quart slow cooker. Add the sliced chicken sausage and broth.

2 Cover and cook on low for 6 hours.

Nutritional Comparison (per serving):

Item	Calories	Fat	Protein	Carbs	Fiber	Effective Carbs
Traditional Chicken and Veggies	199	7.4g	19g	12g	2.3g	9.7g
"Healthified" Chicken and Veggies	185	7.4g	19g	5g	2.3g	2.7g

Roast Chicken

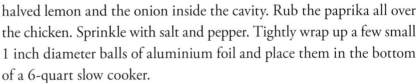

Ingredients:

1 whole chicken

1 lemon, halved

½ c. onion, quartered

1 TBS sweet paprika

Celtic sea salt and pepper to taste

2 c. water or organic chicken broth

Makes 6 servings

Directions:

1 Wash the chicken and place the halved lemon and the onion inside the cavity. Rub the paprika all over the chicken. Sprinkle with salt and pepper. Tightly wrap up a few small 1 inch diameter balls of aluminium foil and place them in the bottom of a 6-quart slow cooker.

2 Pour the water or broth around the aluminium balls. Place the chicken on top of the foil so it isn't touching the bottom. Turn the slow cooker on low for 8-10 hours.

Nutritional Comparison (per serving):

Item	Calories	Fat	Protein	Carbs	Fiber	Effective Carbs
"Healthified" Chicken	188	6g	28.6g	1g	0g	1g

Stuffed Cabbage

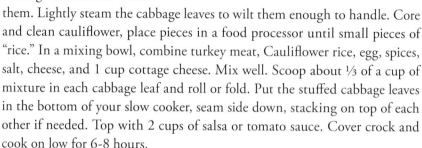

Ingredients:

8 large cabbage leaves

½ c. raw cauliflower "rice"

1 lb ground organic turkey

1 egg

2 tsp onion powder

1 tsp garlic powder

½ tsp Celtic sea salt

⅓ c. shredded Parmesan cheese

1 c. cottage cheese

2 c. salsa or tomato sauce, divided

Directions:

1   Core cabbage, and carefully, peel off large cabbage leaves and wash them. Lightly steam the cabbage leaves to wilt them enough to handle. Core and clean cauliflower, place pieces in a food processor until small pieces of "rice." In a mixing bowl, combine turkey meat, Cauliflower rice, egg, spices, salt, cheese, and 1 cup cottage cheese. Mix well. Scoop about ⅓ of a cup of mixture in each cabbage leaf and roll or fold. Put the stuffed cabbage leaves in the bottom of your slow cooker, seam side down, stacking on top of each other if needed. Top with 2 cups of salsa or tomato sauce. Cover crock and cook on low for 6-8 hours.

Nutritional Comparison (per serving):

Item	Calories	Fat	Protein	Carbs	Fiber	Effective Carbs
Traditional Stuffed Cabbage	481	18g	45g	27.2g	3g	24.2g
"Healthified" Cabbage	399	18g	45g	9.1g	3g	6.1g

Makes 4 servings

Reuben Rolls

Ingredients:

1 large head of cabbage

8 oz. corned beef

2 c. Swiss cheese, shredded

6 c. fermented sauerkraut, divided

8 oz. cream cheese

OPTIONAL:

Stone ground mustard for dipping

Directions:

1   In a pot, boil water and place large leaves of cabbage in the water. Boil for 5-7 minutes or until tender.

2   Place the corned beef in a bowl and shred using two forks; one to hold the beef in place and the other to scrape across the meat. Add cheese, 3 cups sauerkraut, and cream cheese. Mix well and set aside.

3   Lay cabbage tortillas out flat, and evenly distribute corned beef mixture between the centers. Wrap the cabbage tortillas up tightly. Place 3 cups of sauerkraut on the bottom of a 6-quart slow cooker and place the stuffed cabbage rolls on top. Cover and cook on low for 4-6 hours.

Nutritional Comparison (per serving):

Item	Calories	Fat	Protein	Carbs	Fiber	Effective Carbs
Using Corn Tortilla	447	31.5g	22.1g	20.2g	4g	16.2g
Using Cabbage Tortilla	377	30g	22.7g	6.2g	2.1g	4.1g

Makes 8 servings

BBQ Chicken Corn Bread Casserole

Ingredients:

BBQ CHICKEN:

6 frozen skinless, boneless
    chicken breast halves

½ c. onion, diced

2 c. tomato sauce

¼ c. Swerve, Granular
    (or equivalent)

1 tsp liquid smoke

1 tsp Celtic sea salt

"CORN BREAD" TOPPING

1 ¼ c. cottage cheese

5 eggs

½ c. coconut flour

1 tsp baking powder

1 tsp Celtic sea salt

1 tsp Mexican seasoning

Directions:

1   Place the chicken, onion, tomato sauce, natural sweetener, liquid smoke and salt in a greased slow cooker. Cook on medium for 4 hours or until chicken is shreddable. Shred with a fork and spread evenly on the bottom of the slow cooker.

2   Meanwhile, in a food processor or large bowl, mix the cottage cheese, coconut flour, baking powder, eggs, salt and Mexican seasoning until very smooth.

3   Top the shredded chicken with "Corn Bread" topping. Cook on low for an additional 4 hours or until corn bread is cooked through.

Nutritional Comparison (per serving):

Item	Calories	Fat	Protein	Carbs	Fiber	Effective Carbs
Traditional BBQ Pie	305	8g	26.7g	32.4g	0.9g	31.5g
"Healthified" Pie	207	8g	26.7g	5.1g	2g	3.1g

Makes 12 servings

Chicken Caesar Sandwiches

Ingredients:

2 lbs boneless skinless chicken thighs

2 c. organic chicken broth

1 tsp Celtic sea salt

1 tsp fresh ground pepper

½ c. Caesar dressing
    (check for no soybean oil)

½ c. Parmesan cheese, shredded

¼ c. fresh chopped parsley

½ tsp ground pepper

2 c. shredded romaine lettuce

8 "Healthified" buns

"HEALTHIFIED" BUNS:

1 ¼ c. blanched almond flour
    (or ½ c. coconut flour)

4 TBS psyllium husk powder
    (no substitutes)

2 tsp baking powder

1 tsp Celtic sea salt

3 egg whites (8 egg whites if using
    coconut flour)

1 c. BOILING water
    (or MARINARA - for Tomato
    Basil Bread!)

Makes 8 servings

Directions:

1   Place chicken in a 3-4 quart slow cooker with 2 cups chicken broth, 1 tsp salt and 1 tsp pepper, cover and cook on low heat for 4-6 hours.

2   Remove chicken from cooker using a slotted spoon and drain the broth from the slow cooker. Place chicken on a cutting board and shred chicken, discarding any fat.

3   Place chicken back in the cooker and pour dressing (more dressing if desired), Parmesan cheese, parsley, and pepper over the top. Stir until mixed evenly.

4   Cover and cook on high heat for 30 minutes or until mixture is hot.

5   Spoon ¼ cup mixture onto each bun. Top with extra shredded Parmesan cheese and lettuce. Serve with Creamy Fennel (see page 61).

6   **TO MAKE THE BUNS,** preheat the oven to 300 degrees F. In a medium sized bowl, combine the flour, psyllium powder (no substitutes: flaxseed meal won't work), baking powder and salt. Mix until dry ingredients are well combined. Add in the eggs and mix until a thick dough. Add boiling water or marinara in the bowl. Mix until well combined and dough firms up. Form 8 rolls. Bake for 45 to 55 minutes. Remove from the oven and allow the bread cool completely. Cut open with a serrated knife. Store in the freezer for easy addition to meals.

Nutritional Comparison (per serving):

Item	Calories	Fat	Protein	Carbs	Fiber	Effective Carbs
Traditional Chicken	398	14.1g	39g	25.5g	1.3g	24.2g
"Healthified" Chicken	336	13g	40.1g	12g	5.9g	6.1g

Easy Reuben Chicken

Ingredients:

⅔ c. organic mayo

⅓ c. tomato sauce

¼ c. dill pickle relish

2 TBS diced onion

Celtic sea salt and pepper to taste

32 oz. sauerkraut, drained

6 boneless chicken breast

1 TBS mustard, divided

3 oz. Swiss cheese, shredded

Directions:

1 In a medium bowl, combine mayo, tomato sauce, pickle relish, onion, salt and pepper until well combined. Set aside.

2 Layer half the sauerkraut in the bottom of a greased 5-6 quart slow cooker. Drizzle with ⅓ cup of dressing. Place 2 to 3 chicken breasts on top and spread half the mustard over the chicken. Top with the remaining sauerkraut and chicken breasts; drizzle another ⅓ cup of dressing over all and reserve the remaining dressing and mustard for serving.

3 Cover and cook on low for 4 hours, or until chicken is cooked through and tender.

4 To serve, place each breast on a plate. Divide the sauerkraut over top the chicken. Top each with shredded Swiss cheese and a drizzle of the remaining dressing and mustard.

Nutritional Comparison (per serving):

Item	Calories	Fat	Protein	Carbs	Fiber	Effective Carbs
Traditional Chicken	375	22g	29.6g	15g	4.9g	10.1g
"Healthified" Chicken	336	16.2g	29.6g	10g	4.9g	5.1g

Makes 6 servings

Chicken Asparagus Rolls

Ingredients:

½ c. organic mayonnaise

3 TBS Dijon mustard

1 lemon, juiced and zested

2 tsp dried tarragon

1 tsp ground black pepper

½ tsp Celtic sea salt

16 spears fresh asparagus, trimmed

4 skinless, boneless chicken breast halves

2 oz. Provolone cheese, shredded

Directions:

1   In a bowl, mix together the mayonnaise, Dijon mustard, lemon juice, lemon zest, tarragon, salt, and pepper until the mixture is well combined. Set aside.

2   Cook asparagus in a preheated oven at 400 degrees F for 8 minutes or until crisp tender (or in the microwave on High until bright green and just tender, 1 to 1 ½ minutes). Set the asparagus spears aside.

3   Place a chicken breast between two sheets of heavy plastic (resealable freezer bags work well) on a solid, level surface. Firmly pound the chicken breast with the smooth side of a meat mallet to a thickness of about ¼ inch. Repeat with the rest of the chicken breasts. Place ½ ounce of Provolone on each chicken breast, and top the cheese with 4 asparagus spears per breast. Roll the chicken breasts around the asparagus and cheese, place seam sides down, in a 4-quart slow cooker.

4   Pour half of the mayonnaise mixture over each chicken breast. Cover and cook on medium for 4-6 hours or until chicken is cooked and tender. Serve with additional sauce.

Nutritional Comparison (per serving):

Item	Calories	Fat	Protein	Carbs	Fiber	Effective Carbs
Traditional Chicken Rolls	334	16.8g	29g	12g	1.4g	10.6g
"Healthified" Chicken Rolls	316	16.4g	29g	7.4g	1.4g	6g

Makes 4 servings

Cornish Game Hens

Ingredients:

1 small onion, cut in thick slices

4 garlic cloves, minced

1 tsp lemon pepper

½ tsp Celtic sea salt

½ tsp dried basil

1 sprig of rosemary

2 cornish game hens, thawed, skin removed and patted dry

Makes 4 servings

Directions:

1 Place onion slices in bottom of slow cooker.

2 Mix the garlic, lemon pepper, salt, basil and rosemary together. Rub all over the hens. Place hens on top of onion slices (breast side down).

3 Cover and cook on low for 4 to 5 hours. Discard onions and serve.

Nutritional Comparison (per serving):

Item	Calories	Fat	Protein	Carbs	Fiber	Effective Carbs
"Healthified" Game Hens	340	23.4g	29g	1g	0g	1g

Chicken Broccoli Casserole

Ingredients:

6 chicken breasts

8 oz. cream cheese

1 c. organic chicken broth

1 c. organic mayo

4 oz. cheddar cheese, shredded

4 oz. Provolone cheese, shredded

4 c. frozen broccoli, thawed and chopped

Celtic sea salt & pepper to taste

Makes 12 servings

Directions:

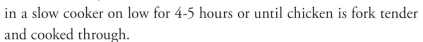

1 Place the chicken, cream cheese, broth and mayo in a slow cooker on low for 4-5 hours or until chicken is fork tender and cooked through.

2 Shred the chicken with a fork. Add the cheeses, broccoli and salt and pepper to taste.

3 Cook on low for an additional hour or until cheese is melted. Serve over Miracle Rice or cauliflower "rice" (see page 17).

Nutritional Comparison (per serving):

Item	Calories	Fat	Protein	Carbs	Fiber	Effective Carbs
Traditional Casserole	388	27.7g	27.5g	7.8g	0.5g	7.3g
"Healthified" Casserole	356	24g	27.8g	7.5g	1g	6.5g

Balsamic Chicken

Ingredients:

1 tsp garlic powder

1 tsp oregano

½ tsp Celtic sea salt

½ tsp freshly ground pepper

2 tsp dried minced onion

8 chicken thighs

4 garlic cloves, minced

½ c. balsamic vinegar

Makes 8 servings

Directions:

1 Combine the first five dry spices in a small bowl and spread over chicken on both sides. Place chicken and garlic in a 4-quart slow cooker. Pour balsamic vinegar over the chicken.

2 Cover and cook on high for 4 hours. If your sauce separates, strain the sauce from the chicken and puree in a food processor until smooth, then pour over chicken.

Nutritional Comparison (per serving):

Item	Calories	Fat	Protein	Carbs	Fiber	Effective Carbs
Traditional Chicken	245	9g	33g	8g	0g	8g
"Healthified" Chicken	223	8g	33g	1.1g	0g	1.1g

OREGANO FACTS:
Benefits Of Oregano:

1 **ANTI-BACTERIAL.** The oils in oregano include thymol and carvacrol, both of which have been shown to inhibit the growth of bacteria, including Pseudomonas aeruginosa and Staphylococcus aureus. Oregano to be more effective against Giardia than the commonly used prescription drug.

2 **ANTI-OXIDANT.** Oregano contains tons of phytonutrients; including thymol and rosmarinic acid. They are potent antioxidants that can prevent oxygen-based free-radical damage to cells. On a per gram fresh weight basis, oregano has demonstrated 42 times more antioxidant activity than apples, 30 times more than potatoes, 12 times more than oranges and 4 times more than blueberries.

3 **PAIN RELIEVER.** Concentrated amounts of oregano can help calm stomach upsets and painful menstruation.

4 **IBS.** Oregano increases the motility of the gastro-intestinal tract as well as increase digestion by increasing gastro-intestinal secretions.

5 **DIABETES/CANCER/CHOLESTEROL.** Oregano is a rich source of fiber, which helps stabilize blood sugar levels. Fiber works in the body to bind to bile salts and cancer-causing toxins in the colon and remove them from the body. This forces the body to break down cholesterol to make more bile salts. These are just some of the reasons that diets high in fiber have been shown to lower high cholesterol levels and reduce the risk of colon cancer.

Jambalaya

Ingredients:

2 c. cauliflower rice

1 lb chicken breasts, 1-inch cubes

½ lb andouille sausage, diced

1 (28-oz.) can diced tomatoes

½ medium onion, chopped

1 green bell pepper, seeded and chopped

1 stalk celery, chopped

1 c. organic chicken broth

2 tsp dried oregano

2 tsp Cajun or Creole seasoning

2 bay leaves

½ tsp dried thyme

1 tsp hot sauce

1 lb frozen peeled and cooked shrimp, thawed

¼ tsp guar gum (thickener)

Makes 8 servings

Directions:

1   Place cauliflower in a food processor and pulse until small pieces of "rice." Set aside (can be done the night before). See page 152 for fried "rice".

2   Place the chicken, sausage, tomatoes, onion, green pepper, celery, and chicken broth in a 4-quart slow cooker. Stir in oregano, Cajun seasoning, hot sauce, bay leaves, and thyme.

3   Cover and cook on low for 7 hours or on high for 3 hours.

4   Just before serving, stir in the thawed shrimp, cover and cook until the shrimp is heated through, about 5 minutes. Whisk in guar gum if desired (to thicken sauce). Discard bay leaves and spoon mixture over stir fried cauliflower "rice" (see page 152).

Nutritional Comparison (per cup):

Item	Calories	Carbs	Fiber
White Rice	242	53g	0g
Brown Rice	218	46g	4g
Cauliflower "Rice"	28	3g	1g

Nutritional Comparison (per serving):

Item	Calories	Fat	Protein	Carbs	Fiber	Effective Carbs
Traditional Jambalaya	472	13g	39g	42g	2.5g	39.5g
"Healthified" Jambalaya	303	13g	36.5g	8.1g	2.5g	5.6g

Chicken Gumbo

Ingredients:

2 c. cauliflower rice

1 lb boneless chicken breasts, cut into 2-inch pieces

1 (10-oz.) package frozen okra, thawed

2 links andouille sausage, diced

1 c. chopped onions

2 celery stalks, chopped

1 green bell pepper, seeded and chopped

1 tsp dried thyme

1 tsp dried oregano

½ tsp Celtic sea salt

2 bay leaves

½ tsp onion powder

½ tsp garlic powder

½ tsp mustard powder

¼ tsp cayenne pepper

¼ tsp ground black pepper

2 c. organic chicken broth

2 c. tomato sauce

Makes 12 servings

Directions:

1. Place cauliflower in a food processor and pulse until small pieces of "rice." Set aside (can be done the night before). See page 152.

2. In a slow cooker, combine the chicken and all remaining ingredients except the cauliflower rice. Mix well to combine.

3. Cover and cook on low for 6 to 8 hours or high for 3 to 4 hours.

4. Discard bay leaves and spoon mixture over stir fried cauliflower rice (see page 152).

Nutritional Comparison (per cup):

Item	Calories	Carbs	Fiber
White Rice	242	53g	0g
Brown Rice	218	46g	4g
Cauliflower "Rice"	28	3g	1g

Nutritional Comparison (per serving):

Item	Calories	Fat	Protein	Carbs	Fiber	Effective Carbs
Traditional Gumbo	301	9.4g	23.9g	28.3g	3g	25.3g
"Healthified" Gumbo	221	9.4g	23.3g	9.7g	3.5g	6.2g

Chicken with Mushroom Cream Sauce

Ingredients:

5 chicken thighs, skin removed

½ c. organic chicken broth

1 TBS coconut aminos OR
   organic Tamari (soy) sauce

2 bay leaves

1 c. green peppers, diced

2 c. chopped baby bella
   mushrooms

¼ c. onion, diced

2 tsp minced garlic

½ tsp dried thyme

1 tsp dried tarragon leaves

½ tsp Celtic sea salt and pepper

1 TBS coconut oil or butter, melted

SAUCE:

3 TBS butter or coconut oil

½ tsp guar gum, thickener

6 TBS heavy cream

Makes 5 servings

Directions:

1   Place chicken, broth, coconut aminos, and bay leaves in bottom of a 4-quart slow cooker.

2   Place peppers, mushrooms, onions and garlic on a cookie sheet and sprinkle with thyme, tarragon, salt and pepper. Drizzle with melted coconut oil or butter. Stir until veggies are coated with the seasonings and oil. Place pan in a 400 degree pre-heated oven. Cook for about 15-20 minutes. Scrape the veggies off the sheet and place onto the top of the chicken.

3   Cover and cook on low for 4-6 hours until chicken is tender. Remove the bay leaves once the chicken is finished.

4   Meanwhile, in a pan melt 3 tablespoons of butter over low heat (it should be frothy). Slowly whisk in the guar gum, it will thicken in a few minutes, don't add more. Slowly add in the juices from the slow cooker (¼ cup at a time). Whisk until the mixture is nice and thick and creamy. Then slowly add in 1 tablespoon of cream at a time. Season with extra tarragon and thyme, if desired. Salt and pepper to taste.

5   Place chicken and mushrooms on individual serving plates and top generously with the creamy sauce. Note: If your sauce separates, strain the sauce from the chicken. Puree in a food processor until smooth. Pour over chicken.

Nutritional Comparison (per serving):

Item	Calories	Fat	Protein	Carbs	Fiber	Effective Carbs
Traditional Chicken	289	23g	18.1g	9g	1g	8g
"Healthified" Chicken	268	19g	18.1g	4.2g	1g	3.2g

Creamed Pheasant

Ingredients:

2 pheasants, cut meat from
    bones, into strips

2 TBS coconut oil

1 bulb of roasted garlic
    (see page 34)

¼ c. chopped onion

1 lb. mushrooms, sliced

½ c. organic chicken broth

½ c. cream cheese

Directions:

1 Clean and rinse the pheasant. Pat dry.

2 Heat oil in a sauté pan until hot. Sear the pheasant in the oil for 2 minutes on each side, to seal in the juices. Remove meat and set aside. Squeeze the roasted bulb of garlic from the stem to squirt the creamy garlic filling in the pan. Also add onion. Sauté until the mushrooms are golden.

3 Remove from heat and pour the contents in the bottom of a 4-quart slow cooker. Place the pheasant on top of the bed of mushrooms. Add the broth and cream cheese in the slow cooker.

4 Cover and cook on low 6-8 hours. After the cream cheese is softened, whisk the mixture to smooth any clumps of cream cheese.

TIP: I keep extra roasted garlic bulbs in the freezer to add lots of flavor to dishes.

Nutritional Comparison (per serving):

Item	Calories	Fat	Protein	Carbs	Fiber	Effective Carbs
Traditional Creamed Pheasant	350	19g	31.9g	11.9g	1g	10.9
"Healthified" Creamed Pheasant	284	15.8g	31.9g	3.5g	1g	2.5g

Makes 6 servings

BBQ Pheasant

Ingredients:

2 lbs pheasant

1 tsp Celtic sea salt

½ c. organic chicken broth

MARINADE:

⅓ c. coconut aminos or organic
  Tamari (soy) sauce

¼ c. onion, minced

1 TBS fish sauce

2 TBS Swerve, Confectioners
  (or equivalent)

2 TBS minced garlic,

1 TBS liquid smoke flavoring

1 TBS Tabasco sauce

3 TBS balsamic vinegar

SAUCE:

1 c. tomato sauce

2 TBS minced onion

1 tsp liquid smoke

½ tsp Celtic sea salt

2 TBS Swerve, Confectioners
  (or equivalent to taste)

Makes 8 servings

Directions:

1   Place pheasant in a large bowl with salt; cover with broth. Let pheasant soak for 1 hour; drain and rinse.

2   Combine the marinade ingredients. Add pheasant and marinate in large non-reactive container and refrigerate for at least 2 hours or overnight. Stir occasionally to keep pheasant coated.

3   Discard marinade and transfer pheasant to slow cooker; add the sauce ingredients. Cover and cook on low for 5 to 7 hours. Serve on "healthified" buns.

Nutritional Comparison (per serving):

Item	Calories	Fat	Protein	Carbs	Fiber	Effective Carbs
Traditional BBQ Pheasant	211	4.2g	26.7g	32g	0g	32g
"Healthified" BBQ Pheasant	159	4.2g	27.2g	1.9g	0g	1.9g

German Pheasant

Ingredients:

6 pheasant breasts

4 c. sauerkraut
  (Bubbies brand is preferred)

½ c. onion, minced

2 c. organic chicken broth

1 tsp Celtic sea salt

½ tsp fresh ground pepper

OPTIONAL:

4 strips bacon, fried until crisp
  and cut into small pieces

1 c. kielbassa (cut into thin disks)
  for additional German flavor

Directions:

1 Place sauerkraut in bottom of a 4-quart slow cooker. Top sauerkraut with the onions and broth. Salt and pepper the pheasant and place pheasant breasts side up on top of sauerkraut and onion.

2 Cover and cook on low for 6-8 hours. The meat will fall off the bone.

SERVING OPTIONS: Serve ½ the meat on a bed of the sauerkraut mix and top with bacon crumbles and sliced kielbassa if desired.

Nutritional Comparison (per serving):

Item	Calories	Fat	Protein	Carbs	Fiber	Effective Carbs
Traditional German Pheasant	177	12.3g	10g	5g	0g	5g
"Healthified" German Pheasant	133	10.3g	10g	0.1g	0g	0.1g

Makes 4 servings

Why Bubbies

Digestive problems? Yeast infections? Chronic Fatigue? Allergies? IBS? Cravings? Eating fermented vegetables daily is a natural cure. If you have a history of using antibiotics, it causes your gut to be more susceptible for parasites and Candida overgrowth. The most common thing I see missing from the majority of diets are fermented foods...no alcohol doesn't count! Nor does grabbing a can of sauerkraut from the shelf at the grocery store. Commercial sauerkraut is preserved in vinegar instead of the traditional lactobacterial probiotics. Instead try making your own or purchasing real fermented products like Bubbies sauerkraut and pickles.

A healthy large intestine is very acidic and has lots of beneficial bacteria such as Lactobacillus acidophilus. These healthy microorganisms feed on the waste left over from our digestion and create lactic acid. We need lactic acid that they produce to keep our colons healthy and in an acidic state. Without them the colon does not have enough acidity to stop the growth of parasites and yeasts and eventually the environment becomes hostile to acidophilus.

Some of the signs of candida yeast overgrowth are fatigue, poor memory, a "spacey" feeling, intense food cravings, gas, loss of sexual desire, bad breath and indigestion. Candida has also been directly linked to allergies, chronic fatigue syndrome, irritable bowel syndrome, multiple chemical sensitivity disorders and various cancers. Use of antibiotics, birth control pills, alcohol and refined foods all increase the risk of developing candida.

We have millions and millions of good gut bacteria in our stomach. But we compromise the good bacteria with over-the-counter medications, antibiotics, diarrhea, colonoscopies, cleanses... All of these can lower the good gut flora. When we are low in good gut flora, serotonin suffers. When we are low in serotonin, we have intense cravings and low moods. Probiotics also protect us from colon cancer, prevention of inflammatory bowel disease, relief from lactose intolerance, diarrhea, and reduction in children's cavities (check out westonaprice.org for proof on this one)!

We need good bacteria for other things too. Most American's are fooled by marketing that we need "whole grains" in order to be healthy. Consuming bacteria helps reduce the phytates and lectins found in grains. These desired microorganisms that create lactic acid in the colon are naturally found in all vegetables and helps turn cabbage into highly-digestible sauerkraut. The fermentation process increases the amount of microorganisms.

Lactic acid also helps digestion at an earlier stage in our stomach. As we get older, our stomach's natural secretions of hydrochloric acid decrease. Hydrochloric acid breaks down food so it can be more easily absorbed by the small intestine. It is also the most important defense we have against harmful bacteria and parasites often present in food. Lactic acid can help compensate for reduced hydrochloric acid.

Unpasteurized sauerkraut and some dairy products such as sour cream (I prefer Horizon's Organic brand) also benefits digestion in the stomach by assisting the pancreas. The pancreas secretes essential digestive enzymes into the stomach. Sauerkraut is especially high in enzymes that work just like the ones from the pancreas.

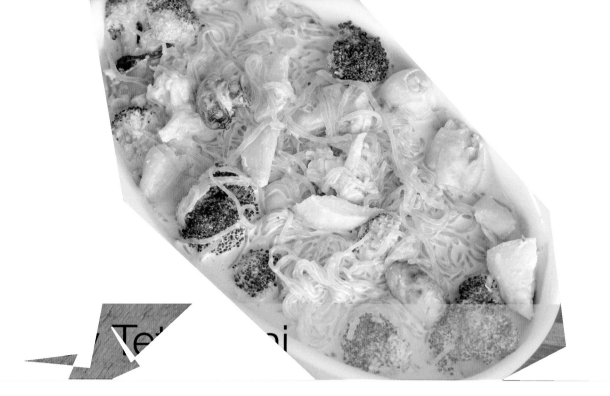

Tetrazzini

Ingredients:

1 pkg Kelp noodles

2 lbs organic turkey or chicken breasts, cut in small chunks

5 oz. sliced mushrooms

1 small onion, diced

1 (14.5-oz.) can artichoke hearts, drained and chopped

1 c. frozen broccoli, chopped

1 (8-oz.) organic cream cheese, chunked

¼ c. shredded Parmesan cheese

2 c. organic chicken broth

½ tsp Celtic sea salt

½ tsp fresh ground pepper

¼ tsp guar gum or xanthan gum (thickener)

Directions:

1 Drain and rinse kelp noodles, cut into 6 inch noodles and place in a 6-quart slow cooker. Top with the raw turkey, mushrooms, onion, artichoke hearts, broccoli, cream cheese, Parmesan, broth, salt and pepper.

2 Cover and cook on low for 6-8 hours.

3 Whisk the mixture so the cream cheese no longer has lumps. Add ¼ tsp guar gum or xanthan gum to thicken if desired.

Nutritional Comparison (per serving):

Item	Calories	Fat	Protein	Carbs	Fiber	Effective Carbs
Traditional Tetrazzini	394	12g	29g	37g	2.3g	34.7g
"Healthified" Tetrazzini	234g	5.3g	27g	5.8g	2.3g	3.5g

Makes 12 servings

Easy White Fish

Ingredients:

4 c. (1 bundle) asparagus

8 (4-oz.) fillets white fish (Mahi Mahi)

1 tsp Celtic sea salt

1 tsp fresh ground pepper

1 TBS cajun seasoning

2 lemons, sliced

2 TBS lemon juice

1 tsp chives, chopped

Directions:

1 Wash the asparagus, and place in a 4-quart slow cooker. Sprinkle the fish with salt, pepper and cajun seasoning. Place the fish and lemon slices on top of the asparagus.

2 Add 2 TBS lemon juice and chives to the slow cooker. Cook on low for about 2-3 hours. Serve with melted butter and lemon slices.

Makes 8 servings

Nutritional Comparison (per serving):

Item	Calories	Fat	Protein	Carbs	Fiber	Effective Carbs
Traditional Mahi Mahi	170	5g	22.6g	7g	1.5g	5.5g
"Healthified" Mahi Mahi	109	0.1g	22.6g	3g	1.5g	1.5g

Lamb with Mint, Rosemary & Garlic

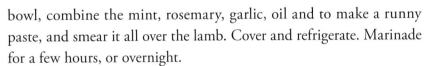

Ingredients:

1 leg of lamb, without the shank

¼ c. fresh mint, chopped

2 TBS fresh rosemary, chopped

4 cloves garlic, crushed

2 TBS macadamia nut or olive oil

1 tsp Celtic sea salt

Directions:

1 Pat the lamb dry. In a medium bowl, combine the mint, rosemary, garlic, oil and to make a runny paste, and smear it all over the lamb. Cover and refrigerate. Marinade for a few hours, or overnight.

2 After marinating, place in a 4-quart slow cooker, add salt and cook on low for 8 hours. Serve hot, with reserved juices from the slow cooker.

Makes 6 servings

Nutritional Comparison (per serving):

Item	Calories	Fat	Protein	Carbs	Fiber	Effective Carbs
"Healthified" Lamb	253	11.2g	32.5g	3.1g	1.5g	1.6g

Deep Dish Pizza

Ingredients:

1 ¼ c. cottage cheese

5 eggs

½ c. coconut flour

1 tsp baking powder

1 tsp Celtic sea salt

TOPPINGS:

Pizza Sauce
  (no soybean oil or sugar)

Sausage, Mushrooms, Peppers

Fresh Mozzarella Cheese

SPICE MIX:

4 TBS Parmesan cheese

3 TBS garlic powder

1 TBS onion powder

1 TBS oregano

Directions:

1 Line a 4-quart slow cooker with parchment paper and grease well. In a food processor or large bowl, mix the cottage cheese, eggs, coconut flour, baking powder, salt and ½ of the spice mix until very smooth.

2 Place dough onto the greased parchment. Top with pizza sauce and your favorite pizza toppings. Sprinkle with spice mix. Turn slow cooker on low for 5-7 hours or until the crust is baked through.

Nutritional Comparison
(per serving of CRUST only):

Item	Calories	Fat	Protein	Carbs	Fiber	Effective Carbs
Traditional Deep Dish Pizza	304	14g	10g	45g	1.2g	43.8g
"Healthified" Deep Dish Pizza	109	4.6g	9.6g	5.2g	2.2g	3g

Makes 9 servings

Italian Eggplant and Goat Cheese

Ingredients:

1 large eggplant

2 c. marinara
(no soybean oil or sugar)

¼ c. almond flour

2 tsp Italian seasoning

½ tsp Celtic sea salt

¼ tsp black pepper

2 egg whites

½ c. goat or feta cheese,
crumbled

Directions:

1 Wash eggplant and slice in ½ inch thick pieces. Pour 1 cup of the marinara in the bottom of a 6-quart slow cooker. Combine almond flour, seasoning, salt and pepper in a shallow dish.

2 In a separate bowl, whip the whites until frothy. Dip eggplant slices in the egg whites, then in the almond flour mixture. Place the eggplant slices on top. Pour the rest of the marinara on top and place the goat or feta over the sauce. Cover and cook on low for 4-6 hours, or high for 3-4.

Nutritional Comparison (per serving):

Item	Calories	Fat	Protein	Carbs	Fiber	Effective Carbs
Traditional Eggplant	198	12g	5g	31g	5.2g	25.8g
"Healthified" Eggplant	132	6g	7.6g	10g	5.5g	4.5g

Makes 4 servings

Italian Stuffed Peppers

Ingredients:

1 lb grass fed ground beef

¼ c. onion, diced

2 cloves garlic, minced

4 c. raw cauliflower "rice"

8 oz. mozzarella or Parmesan cheese, shredded

1 tsp minced fresh parsley

1 tsp Celtic sea salt

¼ tsp freshly ground pepper

6 large red bell peppers, tops cut off and hollowed out

32 oz. crushed tomatoes or marinara sauce

1 ½ c. organic beef broth

Directions:

1 Brown the beef with onions and garlic.

2 Place the ground beef, cauliflower "rice" (see page 17), cheese, parsley, salt and pepper in a large bowl to mix well. Spoon mixture inside peppers, filling to the top. Place stuffed peppers in 5-quart slow cooker. Pour crushed tomatoes and beef broth around the sides.

3 Cover and cook on low for 6 to 8 hours.

Nutritional Comparison (per serving):

Item	Calories	Fat	Protein	Carbs	Fiber	Effective Carbs
Traditional Peppers	531	27g	29g	45g	6g	39g
"Healthified" Peppers	398	15.2g	33g	12g	7g	5g

Makes 6 servings

Pizza Casserole

Ingredients:

4 c. artichoke hearts, drained

4 links organic chicken sausage

8 oz. sliced mushrooms

1 green pepper, sliced

2 c. marinara sauce
(no soybean oils or sugar)

2 c. mozzarella, shredded
(or crumbled goat cheese)

OPTIONAL:
Additional Pizza Toppings, such
as olives

Directions:

1 Place artichokes in a greased slow cooker. Cut up chicken links into ¼ inch pieces. Top with mushrooms, peppers. and marinara sauce.

2 Cover and cook on low for 6-8 hours.

3 Remove cover and top with cheese. Let sit for 5 minutes or until cheese is melted.

Nutritional Comparison (per serving):

Item	Calories	Fat	Protein	Carbs	Fiber	Effective Carbs
Traditional Casserole	393	11g	17g	47.2g	2.2g	45g
"Healthified" Casserole	239	10.6g	18g	12g	6g	6g

Makes 8 servings

Easy Spaghetti

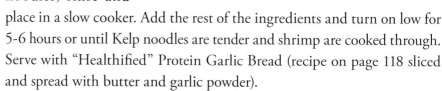

Ingredients:

1 head of cabbage

2 cloves garlic, minced

2 tsp Italian seasoning

4 c. marinara sauce
(no soybean oil or sugar)

Directions:

1   Slice the cabbage into very thin "noodle" shapes. Place all the ingredients in a 4-quart slow cooker.

2   Cover and cook on low for 4-6 hours or until the cabbage is very soft like a noodle.

Makes 12 servings

Nutritional Comparison (per serving):

Item	Calories	Fat	Protein	Carbs	Fiber	Effective Carbs
Traditional Pasta	290	4g	3g	41g	2g	39g
"Healthified" Pasta	91	2.4g	2.5g	11g	4g	7g

Shrimp Scampi

Ingredients:

1 bag Kelp Noodles

½ c. butter or macadamia nut oil

1 TBS Dijon-style mustard

1 TBS fresh lemon juice

1 TBS chopped garlic

1 TBS chopped fresh parsley

1 lb medium raw shrimp
(shell on increases flavor)

Directions:

1   Open the kelp noodles, rinse and place in a slow cooker. Add the rest of the ingredients and turn on low for 5-6 hours or until Kelp noodles are tender and shrimp are cooked through. Serve with "Healthified" Protein Garlic Bread (recipe on page 118 sliced and spread with butter and garlic powder).

Nutritional Comparison (per serving):

Item	Calories	Fat	Protein	Carbs	Fiber	Effective Carbs
Traditional Scampi (using gluten free Rice Noodles)	512	24g	25g	45g	1g	44g
"Healthified" Scampi	320	24g	24.1g	1.1g	0g	1.1g

Makes 4 servings

Chicken Alfredo

Ingredients:

½ c. butter

2 cloves garlic

4 TBS cream cheese

⅓ c. organic beef broth

½ c. Parmesan cheese

4 chicken breasts, cubed

1 package Kelp Noodles

Directions:

1 Place butter in a sauce pan with garlic and cook until light golden brown, stir constantly, or the butter will burn. Turn to a low heat. Smash up garlic cloves in the butter. Stir in cream cheese, broth and Parmesan. Simmer for at least 15 minutes...the flavors open up if you simmer longer:)

2 Place the chicken and rinsed and cut Kelp noodles in a slow cooker on low. Top with alfredo sauce and cook for 4-8 hours or until chicken is cooked through.

3 The longer you let it sit, the softer the noodles get and the more the flavors develop in the sauce.

Nutritional Comparison (per serving):

Item	Calories	Fat	Protein	Carbs	Fiber	Effective Carbs
Traditional Alfredo Pasta	665	33g	17g	71g	trace	71g
"Healthified" Alfredo Pasta	315	31g	7.7g	5.2g	1.3g	3.9g

Makes 4 servings

Protein Lasagna

Ingredients:

1 lb. grass fed hamburger

¼ c. onion, diced

1 clove garlic

2 c. marinara sauce
(no sugar or soybean oil)

1 lb thinly shaved turkey breast

2 c. cottage cheese

3 c. shredded Mozzarella cheese

½ c. Parmesan cheese

Directions:

1 Brown the hamburger with the onion and garlic in a pan and drain. Grease a 6-quart slow cooker. Spread a layer of sauce in bottom of slow cooker. Stir the remaining sauce into hamburger. Place ½ of hamburger in slow cooker. Layer protein "noodles" (shaved turkey breast) over hamburger. Top with ½ of the cottage cheese, spreading evenly. Sprinkle with 1 cup Mozzarella cheese. Top the cheese evenly with ½ the browned hamburger. Then top with protein noodles. Add the rest of the mozzarella cheese and sprinkle Parmesan on top.

2 Cook on low 3-½ to 4-½ hours. Let rest for 1 hour to allow the lasagna to "set." Cut into wedges.

NOTES: 1. When choosing a marinara sauce, look for no soybean oil and no added sugar. 2. You can use ricotta, but the cottage cheese is lower in calories and carbs. 3. Why do I add extra parsley? Parsley is high in vitamin A and C, fiber, potassium, magnesium, calcium, niacin, riboflavin and iron. Surprisingly the leaves also contain a significant amount of protein. Parsley is great for the digestive system, freshens the breath and has been traditionally used to relieve intestinal gas. 4. There will be some liquid in the bottom of the slow cooker. The juices pretty much absorb by the next day. Leftover lasagna is so much better anyway!

Nutritional Comparison (per serving):

Item	Calories	Fat	Protein	Carbs	Fiber	Effective Carbs
Traditional Lasagna	361	12.2g	30.1g	30.7g	1.1g	29.6g
"Healthified" Lasagna	294	12.2g	32.6g	5.3g	2g	3.3g

Makes 12 servings

Veggie Lasagna

Ingredients:

1 large eggplant

3 zucchini squash

1 lb mushrooms, sliced

4 c. marinara sauce
(no sugar or soybean oil)

2 c. organic ricotta or
cottage cheese

2 c. mozzarella cheese, shredded

2 c. Parmesan cheese, freshly
grated

Directions:

1   Wash all of the vegetables. Peel and slice the zucchini and the eggplant in long, slices, about ¼ inch thick. These are going to be your noodles! In the bottom of a 4-quart slow cooker, pour about 1 cup marinara sauce. Layer with squash and eggplant "noodles". Evenly place 1 cup ricotta cheese on top. Sprinkle mushrooms on top of the ricotta and then a few slices of mozzarella cheese. Pour in some more marinara sauce. Continue layering the ingredients until you have run out of ingredients. Finish the top with marinara sauce and the freshly grated Parmesan cheese.

2   Cover and cook on low for 5-8 hours. This is done when the vegetables have reached their desired tenderness and the cheese is melted. Let sit for at least 1 hour to let the juices soak into the vegetables or there will be liquid at the bottom of the slow cooker.

Nutritional Comparison (per serving):

Item	Calories	Fat	Protein	Carbs	Fiber	Effective Carbs
Traditional Lasagna	447	12g	21g	58.2g	4g	54.2g
"Healthified" Lasagna	256	11.3g	19.5g	10g	4g	6g

Makes 12 servings

Moussaka

Ingredients:

EGGPLANT LAYER:
3 large eggplants
Pinch of Celtic sea salt and pepper

MEAT LAYER:
½ c. onion, chopped
2 garlic cloves, minced
1 handful fresh oregano leaves, chopped
2 handfuls fresh flat-leaf parsley, chopped
1 ½ lbs ground lamb or beef
2 c. finely chopped mushrooms
½ tsp Celtic sea salt and pepper
¼ tsp nutmeg
1 cinnamon stick
1 (16-oz.) can Contadina Thick and Zesty Tomato Sauce

CHEESE SAUCE:
4 TBS Butter
½ c. organic beef broth
2 eggs, separated
8 oz. feta cheese, crumbled
1 to 2 c. freshly grated Parmesan
Pinch of nutmeg

Makes 8 servings

Directions:

1   Preheat oven to 350 degrees F. Prepare eggplant into ½ inch thick slices, lay on greased cookie sheet, sprinkle with salt and bake in oven for 15 minutes or until soft.

2   MEAT LAYER: Add oil to a sauté pan and toss in the onion, garlic, oregano, and parsley. Cook and stir until soft and fragrant, about 3 minutes. Add the ground lamb and mushrooms (this will "lighten" the dish) stirring to break up the meat; season with salt, pepper and nutmeg, and toss in the cinnamon stick. Stir in the tomato sauce. Simmer until the liquid has evaporated, stirring occasionally. Remove from the heat.

3   In a saucepan, combine 4 TBS butter and broth; cook over low heat. Beat egg yolks, and combine with cheese and nutmeg; add to saucepan. Beat egg whites until stiff and fold into sauce. Remove from heat.

4   Line the bottom of a 6-quart slow cooker with ⅓ of the eggplant slices; they should completely cover the bottom. Spread ½ of the meat sauce over the eggplant, evening it out with a spatula. Sprinkle with ½ of the cheese sauce. Repeat the layers again, ending with a final layer of eggplant. Cover the top with a nice even layer of Parmesan cheese.

5   Cover and cook on low for 6 to 8 hours. Let cool 10 minutes before serving.

Nutritional Comparison (per serving):

Item	Calories	Fat	Protein	Carbs	Fiber	Effective Carbs
Traditional Moussaka	416	24g	13g	37g	9g	28g
"Healthified" Moussaka	421	23.3g	37.6g	16.9g	7.5g	9.4g

Chicken Picatta

Ingredients:

4 boneless chicken breast

½ c. coconut flour

½ tsp pepper

½ tsp garlic powder

1 lemon, zested

Coconut oil

2 tbs. butter

¼ c. lemon juice

1 c. organic chicken stock

2 cloves chopped garlic

¼ c. capers

1 c. fresh mushrooms

1 c. artichoke hearts

½ c. fresh diced cherry tomatoes

Directions:

1   Combine coconut flour, ground pepper, garlic powder and zest of one lemon in shallow dish.

2   Pound out chicken about ¼ inch thick. Heat a few tablespoons of coconut oil on medium-high in a sauté pan. Once the pan is hot, dredge the chicken in the coconut flour mixture and brown both sides in the pan, which will take about 3 minutes on each side.

3   Remove the chicken from the pan and place in a 4-quart slow cooker, adding the remaining ingredients on top of it.

4   Cook on low at 4-6 hours, or until chicken is tender, depends on your slow cooker. Serve over your favorite "healthified" pasta (see page 18) or "healthified" rice (see page 17) if desired.

Nutritional Comparison (per serving):

Item	Calories	Fat	Protein	Carbs	Fiber	Effective Carbs
Traditional Picatta	507	18g	46g	37g	3g	34g
"Healthified" Picatta	402	18g	44.9g	14g	7.6g	6.3g

Makes 4 servings

Chicken Cacciatore

Ingredients:

2 lb boneless chicken breasts

½ tsp Celtic sea salt

¼ tsp pepper

1 c. green bell pepper, chopped

1 c. onion, chopped

1 rib celery, diced

4 oz. mushrooms, sliced

1 (14.5-oz.) can diced tomatoes, undrained

3 cloves garlic, minced

1 tsp basil

1 tsp oregano

1 bay leaf

1 (6-oz.) can tomato paste

¾ c. organic chicken broth

2 TBS balsamic vinegar

½ tsp guar gum
   (optional thickener)

2 c. chopped fresh spinach

Celtic sea salt and pepper to taste

Makes 12 servings

Directions:

1   Season chicken with ½ tsp salt and ¼ tsp pepper. Place chicken in a 6-quart slow cooker. Add the green pepper, onion, celery, mushrooms, tomatoes, garlic, bay leaf, basil and oregano.

2   In a small bowl, combine the tomato paste, chicken broth and balsamic vinegar and guar gum. Mix well. Pour on top of chicken. Cover and cook on low for 8 hours or until the chicken is tender. Remove and discard bay leaf.

3   Add the chopped spinach. Stir and allow to cook for another 20 minutes on high or until the sauce has thickened. Season with additional salt and pepper to taste. Serve over "healthified" pasta (see page 18) or rice (see page 19) if desired.

Nutritional Comparison (per serving):

Item	Calories	Fat	Protein	Carbs	Fiber	Effective Carbs
Traditional Cacciatore	389	9g	34.7g	39g	1g	38g
"Healthified" Cacciatore	246	8.8g	34.7g	5.4g	1.5g	3.9g

Chicken Parmesan

Ingredients:

4 c. marinara sauce
   (no sugar or soybean oil)

1 egg

¼ c. Parmesan cheese

½ tsp Italian Seasoning

¼ tsp Celtic sea salt

¼ tsp black pepper

4 boneless, skinless chicken
   breast halves

Coconut oil for frying

4 oz. fresh mozzarella cheese

Directions:

1   Pour 2 cups marinara sauce in a 4-quart slow cooker. In a medium bowl, whip the egg with a fork. In a separate bowl, combine the Parmesan, Italian seasoning, salt and pepper. Pound out chicken about ¼ inch thick. Dip the chicken in the egg, then in the Parmesan mixture, coating both sides.

2   Heat a few tablespoons of coconut oil on medium-high in a sauté pan. Once the pan is hot, place the coated chicken in the pan and brown both sides in the pan, which will take about 3 minutes on each side.

3   Remove the chicken from the pan and place in a 4-quart slow cooker, adding the marinara on top. Cook on low at 4-6 hours, or until chicken is tender depends on your slow cooker. Serve over your favorite "healthified" pasta if desired.

Nutritional Comparison (per serving):

Item	Calories	Fat	Protein	Carbs	Fiber	Effective Carbs
Traditional Chicken Parm	480	19g	30g	46g	5g	41g
"Healthified" Chicken Parm	277	11.5g	35.2g	6.8g	1.1g	5.7g

Makes 8 servings

Creamy Italian Chicken

Ingredients:

2 lbs uncooked frozen
  chicken breast

32 oz. marinara
  (no sugar or soybean oil)

8 oz. cream cheese

Directions:

1 Put frozen chicken breasts in slow cooker, cover with marinara. Cook on high 4-5 hours or until chicken is cooked.

2 Place block of cream cheese on top. Cook for an additional 30 minutes.

3 Whisk to incorporate cream cheese into sauce. The stirring will cause the chicken to shred.

4 Serve on a "healthified" bun (see page 118).

Nutritional Comparison (per serving):

Item	Calories	Fat	Protein	Carbs	Fiber	Effective Carbs
Traditional Chicken	490	17.6g	40g	42g	3.3g	38.7g
"Healthified" Chicken	349	17.4g	37.3g	8g	2.8g	5.2g

Makes 6 servings

EASY Greek Chicken

Ingredients:

2 lbs chicken thighs or breasts

1 (14.5-oz.) jar fire roasted tomatoes

1 (14.5-oz.) jar marinated sweet
  peppers

½ c. pitted green olives

¼ c. tightly packed basil leaves

8 oz. crumbled feta cheese

Directions:

1 Use a 4-quart slow cooker. Place the chicken on the bottom of your cooker, add the tomatoes, drained marinaded peppers, green olives, basil leaves and crumble on the feta cheese.

2 Cover, and cook on low for 6-7 hours, or on high for about 3 hours. NOTE: If you use frozen chicken, increase the time about 45 minutes.

Nutritional Comparison (per serving):

Item	Calories	Fat	Protein	Carbs	Fiber	Effective Carbs
Traditional Chicken	412	14.7g	38g	32g	2g	30g
"Healthified" Chicken	321	14.7g	38g	6.5g	1.4g	5.1g

Makes 8 servings

Coq Au-No Vin

Ingredients:

6 slices bacon

8 oz. baby portabella
  mushrooms, sliced

1 c. yellow onion, diced

3 cloves garlic, minced

8 frozen chicken thighs or legs

½ tsp black pepper

½ tsp Celtic sea salt

½ c. organic chicken broth

¼ c. red or white wine vinegar

2 TBS Swerve, Granular
  (or equivalent to taste)

2 sprigs of fresh thyme

"FAUX"TATOES
See page 61

Directions:

1   Place the bacon, mushrooms, onions and garlic in a sauté pan and fry until the bacon is cooked. Crumble the bacon. Place the frozen chicken in slow cooker and layer the rest of the ingredients on top.

2   Cover and cook on low for 8 hours. The lower the heat the better for tender chicken with lots of flavor. Serve with mashed "faux"atoes or your favorite "healthified" pasta.

WHY NO ALCOHOL? I'm not concerned about the calories in the alcohol. It is more about how it affects fat oxidation.

Using wine vinegar and a little natural sweetener creates the wine flavor you are looking for in this dish.

Nutritional Comparison (per serving):

Item	Calories	Fat	Protein	Carbs	Fiber	Effective Carbs
Traditional Coq Au Vin	290	17g	20.2g	9g	0.6g	8.4g
"Healthified" Coq Au Vin	244g	17g	20.2g	2.9g	0.6g	1.3g

Makes 12 servings

Orange Spanish Chicken

Ingredients:

4 large chicken breast halves

½ tsp Celtic sea salt

¼ tsp black pepper

2 cloves chopped garlic

½ tsp dried thyme

3 bell peppers, sliced

1 medium yellow onion, sliced in rings

12 large green olives, whole or chopped

½ c. water or organic broth

2 orange tea bags

Makes 4 servings

Directions:

1   Place chicken (frozen is fine) in a 4-quart slow cooker. Add all of the dried spices, peppers, onion, garlic and olives to the slow cooker. Pour in water or broth and add the tea bags.

2   Cover and cook on low for 6-8 hours. Remove the tea bags and serve over Miracle Rice or cauliflower "rice" (see page 17).

Nutritional Comparison (per serving):

Item	Calories	Fat	Protein	Carbs	Fiber	Effective Carbs
Traditional Orange Chicken	355	12g	43g	14g	2.5g	11.5g
"Healthified" Orange Chicken	332g	12g	43g	8g	2.5g	5.5g

Pesto Fish

Ingredients:

2 lbs white fish (Sole or Cod)

1 tsp Celtic sea salt

½ tsp fresh ground pepper

1 (4-oz.) bottle pesto (no soybean oil)

OPTIONAL:

½ c. Goat cheese or Parmesan cheese, shredded

Makes 6 servings

Directions:

1   Lay a piece of foil on a clean working area. Place a piece of fish on it. Season the fish with salt and pepper. Cover it with a spoonful of pesto. If desired, sprinkle on some goat cheese or freshly shredded Parmesan. Fold the foil to create a packet. Place the packet in a 4-quart slow cooker. Repeat with remaining fish.

2   OPTIONAL: Add a layer of asparagus, spinach, squash, zucchini, or another low starch veggie you desire in the bottom of each packet of fish.

3   Cover and cook on low for 3-4 hours. The fish is done when it is fully white and flakes nicely with a fork.

Nutritional Comparison (per serving):

Item	Calories	Fat	Protein	Carbs	Fiber	Effective Carbs
Traditional Fish	191	7.9g	26g	1.2g	0g	1.2g
"Healthified" Fish	191	7.9g	26g	1.2g	0g	1.2g

Chicken Cordon Bleu

Ingredients:

4 (4-oz.) chicken breasts

8 (1-oz.) slices of ham or turkey

4 oz. swiss cheese, sliced

1 TBS organic butter

3 TBS cream cheese

½ c. organic chicken broth

¼ tsp Celtic sea salt

¼ tsp black pepper

Directions:

1   Grease a 4-quart slow cooker. Place the chicken in a Ziplock bag and pound breasts flat. Put 2 slices of the ham and a slice of swiss cheese on the chicken breast and roll it up. Set the rolled chicken in the slow cooker, seam side down. Continue the process until all the chicken is stuffed and placed in the slow cooker.

2   To make your sauce, whisk the butter, cream cheese, broth, salt and pepper in a small saucepan and stir until cream cheese is melted and you have a smooth sauce. Pour on top of the chicken.

3   Cover and cook on low for 6-8 hours or until the chicken is cooked all the way through.

Nutritional Comparison (per serving):

Item	Calories	Fat	Protein	Carbs	Fiber	Effective Carbs
Traditional Cordon Bleu	556	25.2g	51g	26.6g	0.6g	26g
"Healthified" Cordon Bleu	426	23g	50.3g	1.8g	0g	1.8g

Makes 4 servings

Take Out Beef and Broccoli

Ingredients:

1 c. organic beef broth

½ c. coconut aminos or organic Tamari (soy) sauce

⅓ c. Swerve, Confectioners (or equivalent)

1 TBS sesame oil

4 garlic cloves, minced

¼ c. onion, diced

¼ c. scallions, diced

2 TBS grated ginger

½ tsp guar gum (thickener)

1 lb. boneless, grass fed beef chuck roast, sliced into thin strips

4 c. frozen broccoli flowerettes

Celtic sea salt and pepper to taste

2 c. cauliflower rice (see page 17), cooked OR Miracle Rice, rinsed

Makes 4 servings

Directions:

1   Place the beef broth, organic Tamari sauce, sweetener, sesame oil, garlic, onion, scallions, ginger and guar gum in a 4-quart slow cooker and whisk until combined. Gently place slices of beef in the liquid and toss to coat. Turn slow cooker on low and cook for 4 to 6 hours. Toss in broccoli flowerettes and cook for an additional 30 minutes or until broccoli is tender. Add salt and pepper to taste. Serve hot over "healthified rice". Add another ½ tsp guar gum to thicken if desired.

2   TO MAKE THE "RICE," cut the cauliflower into pieces and pulse in a food processor until it is the consistency of small pieces of "rice." TIP: You can also use the heart of the cauliflower for rice, or use for making "French Fries." (TIP: can do this up to 2 days ahead of time and store in fridge for easy lunch/dinner options). Stir fry the cauliflower "rice" for about 3-5 minutes or until cauliflower pieces are done to desired liking.

3   HELPFUL COOKING TIP: All slow cooker temperatures differ a bit, yours may differ in temperature than mine, I suggest cooking this for 4 hours on your first attempt. 6 hours will most likely make "shredded" beef instead of slices, so decrease cooking time by 2 hours if desired.

Nutritional Comparison (per serving):

Item	Calories	Fat	Protein	Carbs	Fiber	Effective Carbs
Traditional Beef and Broccoli	524	11g	40g	61.5g	3.4g	51.8g
"Healthified" Beef and Broccoli	281	11g	37.9g	6.8g	3g	3.8g

5-Spice Steak

Ingredients:

1 lb thin flank steak

¼ tsp Celtic sea salt

1 tsp Five-Spice Powder

½ tsp ground ginger

¼ tsp black pepper

6 cloves garlic, minced

2 TBS coconut aminos OR
    organic Tamari (soy) sauce

1 TBS coconut or white wine
    vinegar

Directions:

1   In a small bowl, mix the dry spices. Rub the mixture on all sides of the meat. Place the steak in a ziplock bag and add the garlic, coconut aminos/Tamari sauce, and vinegar. Seal the bag and refrigerate overnight.

2   Place the marinaded steak in a 4-quart slow cooker and cook on low for 4-5 hours.

3   Remove from slow cooker. Slice the steak into thin strips and serve over a bed of organic greens or low starch vegetable.

Makes 4 servings

Nutritional Comparison (per serving):

Item	Calories	Fat	Protein	Carbs	Fiber	Effective Carbs
"Healthified" Steak	232	9.9g	31.9g	1.9g	0g	1.9g

Thai Beef and Pasta Salad

Ingredients:

1 c. onion thinly sliced in rings

1 ½ lb. flank steak, trimmed & patted dry

4 cloves garlic, minced

¼ c. Swerve, Confectioners
(or equivalent)

⅓ c. coconut aminos OR organic Tamari
(soy) sauce

3 TBS freshly squeezed lime juice

2 TBS peeled and minced fresh ginger

1 tsp toasted sesame oil

1/2 tsp pepper

2 pkg. Miracle Noodles (fettuccine
shape) OR 1 package Kelp noodles

DRESSING:

¼ c. rice wine vinegar

4 tsp coconut aminos OR organic
Tamari (soy) sauce

1 tsp ginger juice
(from grated, squeezed ginger)

1 tsp toasted sesame oil

4 tsp Thai sweet chili sauce

½ tsp cayenne pepper

2 limes, juiced

14 fresh mint leaves, chopped

1 bunch green onions, chopped

¼ c. cilantro, finely chopped

1 bunch water cress

¼ c. sunflower seeds or chopped peanuts

Makes 12 servings

Directions:

1   Grease a 6-quart slow cooker and place the onion slices on bottom. Make shallow horizontal slits against the grain across the top of the steak, lay on onion. In small bowl, combine garlic, natural sweetener, coconut aminos/Tamari, lime juice, ginger, sesame oil and pepper. Pour over steak, coating all surfaces. If using Kelp noodles, drain, rinse and set in slow cooker.

2   Cook on low 5-6 hours or until Kelp noodles are very soft. If using Miracle Noodles, drain, rinse and set aside.

3   **TO MAKE THE DRESSING,** combine the vinegar, 4 tsp coconut aminos/Tamari, ginger juice, 1 tsp sesame oil, chili sauce, cayenne, lime juice, mint, green onions, and cilantro in a jar and shake. Refrigerate until meat is done.

4   Let meat stand 10 minutes before cutting across the grain in ½" thick slices. Make a bed of water cress, top with noodles and sliced meats, sprinkle with sunflower seeds or nuts.

Nutritional Comparison (per serving):

Item	Calories	Fat	Protein	Carbs	Fiber	Effective Carbs
Traditional Beef Salad	273	7g	18g	30.6g	0.6g	30g
"Healthified" Beef Salad	140	6g	16.6g	3.3g	1.8g	1.5g

Korean Short Ribs

Ingredients:

½ c. coconut aminos OR organic Tamari (soy) sauce

⅓ c. Swerve, Confectioners (or equivalent)

¼ c. rice vinegar

2 cloves garlic, peeled and smashed

1 TBS grated fresh ginger

½ tsp crushed red pepper

8 (4 lbs) grass fed beef short ribs

1 green cabbage, quartered

½ tsp guar gum (thickener)

1 TBS sesame oil

4 scallions, thinly sliced

Directions:

1   In a 4- to 6-quart slow cooker, combine the coconut aminos/Tamari sauce, natural sweetener, vinegar, garlic, ginger, and red pepper. Add the short ribs, arranging in a single layer. Lay the cabbage on top.

2   Cook, covered, on low for 7 to 8 hours until the meat is tender and easily pulls away from the bone.

3   Transfer the cabbage and short ribs to plates. With a large spoon or ladle, skim the fat from the cooking liquid and discard, but keep the cooking liquid in the slow cooker. Turn the slow cooker to high.

4   In a small bowl, whisk together the guar gum with 1 tablespoon of water until smooth. Whisk into the cooking liquid and cook until thickened, 2 to 3 minutes. Stir in the sesame oil. Spoon the sauce over the short ribs and cabbage and sprinkle with the scallions.

NOTE: Most rice vinegars have sugar added to them, please read labels. STAR Rice Vinegar brand has no sugar.

Nutritional Comparison (per serving):

Item	Calories	Fat	Protein	Carbs	Fiber	Effective Carbs
Traditional Ribs	631	14g	21g	31g	2.5g	28.5g
"Healthified" Ribs	469	14g	21g	6.5g	2.5g	4g

Makes 4 servings

Garlic Chicken Fried "Rice"

Ingredients:

¼ c. onion, sliced

1 whole chicken (3 pounds)

1 TBS butter or coconut oil

¼ tsp Celtic sea salt

1 tsp smoked paprika

¼ tsp fresh ground pepper

20 garlic cloves, peeled, but intact

FRIED "RICE"

⅓ c. chopped onion

1 clove garlic

2 TBS butter or coconut oil

4 c. cauliflower, into rice

3 TBS coconut aminos OR
    organic Tamari (soy sauce)

2 TBS minced fresh parsley

⅛ tsp pepper

1 egg, lightly beaten

Directions:

1 Prepare a 6-quart oval slow cooker. Place onion slices on the bottom of the insert. In a large mixing bowl, mix butter/oil, salt, paprika and pepper. Rub mix over chicken. Place chicken and garlic in slow cooker, on top of the onion. Tip: do not add water.

2 Cover and cook on low for 6-8 hours. The longer you cook chicken-on-the-bone, the more tender it will be. Place the drumsticks towards the inside of the stoneware, or they will stick to the sides and burn. When chicken is done, remove meat from the bones and set aside.

3 Serve with cauliflower Fried "Rice." Place cauliflower flowerettes in a food processor. Pulse until small pieces of "rice." In a skillet, sauté onion and garlic in butter until tender. Stir in the cauliflower rice, Tamari sauce, parsley and pepper. Cook over medium-low heat for 5 minutes, stirring occasionally. Add the egg; cook and stir until egg is completely set, about 3 minutes. Mix with reserved chicken. Garnish with green onion if desired.

Nutritional Comparison (per serving):

Item	Calories	Fat	Protein	Carbs	Fiber	Effective Carbs
Traditional Fried Rice	301	7g	6g	41.7g	1g	40.7g
"Healthified" Fried Rice	106	7g	5.1g	7.3g	3g	4.3g

Makes 4 servings

Yakisoba Chicken

Ingredients:

2 inches fresh ginger

½ head green cabbage

1 stalk broccoli

1 medium yellow onion

1 large chicken breast

2 TBS coconut oil

1 tsp sesame oil

¼ c. coconut aminos OR organic
    Tamari (soy) sauce

¼ c. organic chicken broth

2 TBS tomato sauce

1 tsp to 1 TBS hot sauce

1 TBS Swerve, Confectioners
    (or equivalent)

2 packages Miracle or
    Kelp noodles

Directions:

1   Peel the ginger with either a vegetable peeler or the side of a spoon and then grate it with a cheese grater. Remove the core from the cabbage and cut into thin strips (like 'noodles'). Slice the onion in thin strips. Cut the broccoli in bite-sized pieces. Slice the chicken in thin strips. Place in a greased slow cooker with the coconut oil and sesame oil.

2   In a small bowl, combine the coconut aminos/Tamari sauce, broth, tomato sauce, hot sauce and natural sweetener. Add hot sauce to your desired heat liking. Add the sauce to the slow cooker and cook on medium heat for 6-8 hours or until chicken and veggies are cooked through.

3   Rinse and drain the Miracle Noodles. Place the noodles in the pot and stir. Heat through and serve.

NOTE: In this comparison, all I changed was switching the gluten free Rice Noodles to Miracle Noodles!

Makes 8 servings

Nutritional Comparison (per serving):

Item	Calories	Fat	Protein	Carbs	Fiber	Effective Carbs
Traditional Yakisoba	292	5.3g	9g	50.1g	3g	47.1g
"Healthified" Yakisoba	102	5g	8.3g	6.3g	2.1g	4.2g

Thai Chicken Thighs

Ingredients:

8 skinless chicken thighs

1 c. salsa (no sugar)

½ c. sunbutter or natural peanut butter

4 TBS Swerve, Confectioners (or equivalent)

2 TBS coconut aminos OR organic Tamari (soy) sauce

3 TBS lime juice

2 TBS fresh cilantro, diced

2 tsp ginger, grated

Makes 8 servings

Directions:

1 Place chicken, salsa, nut butter, natural sweetener, coconut aminos/Tamari, lime juice, fresh cilantro and grated ginger in a 5-quart slow cooker and set on low for 6 hours. Serve warm over cauliflower rice (see page 17) or Miracle rice.

Nutritional Comparison (per serving):

Item	Calories	Fat	Protein	Carbs	Fiber	Effective Carbs
Traditional Thai Chicken	332	12.2g	41.1g	15.5g	1.6g	13.9g
"Healthified" Thai Chicken	293	12.2g	41.1g	6g	1.6g	4.4g

General Tso's Chicken

Ingredients:

1 lb boneless, skinless chicken, cut in strips

4 garlic cloves, minced

3 TBS Swerve, Confectioners (or equivalent to taste)

1 tsp freshly grated ginger

2 TBS coconut aminos OR organic Tamari (soy) sauce

½ tsp crushed red pepper flakes

1 (16-oz.) package frozen broccoli

Makes 4 servings

Directions:

1 Place the chicken on the bottom of a 4-quart slow cooker. Add the garlic, natural sweetener, ginger, coconut aminos/Tamari sauce, and red pepper flakes. Stir the chicken to fully coat with the sauce. Cover and cook on low for 5 to 6 hours, then add the frozen broccoli. Cover and cook on high for an hour, or until the broccoli is fully hot and the chicken is very tender.

2 Serve with cauliflower "rice" (see page 17) or Miracle Rice.

Nutritional Comparison (per serving):

Item	Calories	Fat	Protein	Carbs	Fiber	Effective Carbs
Traditional Chicken	259	3.9g	36.3g	18.5g	3g	15.5g
"Healthified" Chicken	218	3.9g	36.3g	8g	3g	5g

Sesame Chicken

Ingredients:

2 lbs boneless, skinless chicken thighs or 4 chicken breasts

Celtic sea salt and pepper to taste

½ c. onion, minced

2 cloves garlic, minced

1 c. Nature's Hollow Xylitol Honey (or Swerve, Confectioners)

¼ c. tomato sauce

½ c. coconut aminos OR organic Tamari (soy) sauce

2 TBS melted coconut oil or macadamia oil

¼ tsp red pepper flakes

½ tsp guar gum (thickener)

⅓ c. organic broth or water

OPTIONAL:

2 packages Miracle Rice

1 TBS sesame seeds

3 scallions, chopped

Makes 4 servings

Directions:

1   Place chicken in a 6-quart slow cooker and lightly season both sides with salt and pepper. In a medium bowl, combine onion, garlic, natural sweetener, tomato sauce, coconut aminos/Tamari, oil and red pepper flakes. Pour over chicken. Cook on low for 3-4 hours. Remove chicken to a cutting board, leaving sauce. Shred chicken in bite-sized pieces; set aside. Drain and rinse Miracle Rice (or prepare cauliflower "rice" see page 17).

2   In a small bowl, dissolve guar gum in ⅓ cup broth or water; add to slow cooker. Stir to combine with sauce. Cover and cook sauce on high for ten more minutes, or until slightly thickened.

3   Place the "rice" onto 4 plates, top with chicken and spoon sauce over top. Sprinkle evenly with sesame seeds and chopped scallions.

Nutritional Comparison (per serving):

Item	Calories	Fat	Protein	Carbs	Fiber	Effective Carbs
Stouffer's Sesame Chicken	590	16g	25.1g	87g	6g	81g
"Healthified" Sesame Chicken	190	8.7g	24.3g	4g	1.1g	2.9g

Cashew Chicken

Ingredients:

2 lbs boneless, skinless chicken
   breasts

SAUCE:

¼ c. coconut aminos OR organic
   Tamari sauce

2 TBS rice wine vinegar

2 TBS tomato paste

2 TBS Swerve, Confectioners
   (or equivalent)

1 garlic clove, minced

½ tsp grated fresh ginger

¼ tsp red pepper flakes

GARNISH:

½ c. cashews

Directions:

1 Place chicken in a 4-quart slow cooker. Combine coconut aminos/ Tamari sauce, vinegar, tomato paste, natural sweetener, garlic, ginger, and pepper flakes in small bowl; pour over chicken. If you would like extra sauce, double the sauce ingredients.

2 Cook on low for 3 to 4 hours. Add cashews and stir. Serve over "healthified" cauliflower "rice" (see page 17) or miracle rice.

Nutritional Comparison (per serving):

Item	Calories	Fat	Protein	Carbs	Fiber	Effective Carbs
Traditional Cashew Chicken	493	16.7g	48g	48g	0.8g	47.2g
"Healthified" Cashew Chicken	364	16.5g	46g	5.2g	0.6g	4.6g

Makes 6 servings

Chicken Adobo

Ingredients:

2 shallots, minced

6 cloves garlic, minced

3 TBS Swerve, Confectioners
(or equivalent to taste)

¼ tsp cayenne pepper

½ tsp pepper

2 bay leaves

½ c. chicken stock

⅓ c. coconut aminos OR organic
Tamari (soy) sauce

¼ c. coconut or apple cider
vinegar

2 lbs chicken thighs

"Healthified" rice, for serving

Directions:

1 In a 4-quart slow cooker, place the shallots, garlic, natural sweetener, cayenne, black pepper and bay leaves. Add the chicken stock, Tamari sauce, vinegar and chicken. Gently mix to combine the chicken with the mixture. Cover and cook on low heat for 6 hours.

2 Preheat the oven to broil. Place a cooling rack inside a baking sheet lined with foil. Remove the chicken thighs from the slow cooker and place onto the prepared baking sheet. Strain the remaining sauce in a pot and cook over medium high heat, stirring frequently, until reduced by half, about 8-10 minutes. Brush both sides of each chicken thigh with the sauce. Place in oven and broil for 2-3, or until slightly charred and crispy. Serve with "healthified" rice (see page 17) or Miracle rice, if desired.

Nutritional Comparison (per serving):

Item	Calories	Fat	Protein	Carbs	Fiber	Effective Carbs
Traditional Chicken Adobo	499	12.7g	45g	45.1g	1g	44.1g
"Healthified" Chicken Adobo	306	12.2g	44.2g	1.8g	0g	1.8g

Makes 6 servings

Chicken on Curry "Rice"

Ingredients:

CHICKEN:

2 lbs chicken breasts, cut in
½-inch pieces

2 TBS curry powder

½ c. onion, thinly sliced

2 cloves garlic, crushed

1 (14-oz.) can coconut milk

2 red peppers, sliced

1 (8-oz.) can tomato sauce

¼ c. Swerve, Confectioners
(or equivalent)

1 tsp Celtic sea salt

½ tsp pepper

1 ½ TBS coconut oil

RICE:

4 c. cauliflower, pulsed into rice

2 TBS coconut oil

1 TBS minced garlic

1 TBS ground cumin

1 TBS ground curry powder

1 TBS chili powder

1 c. organic chicken broth

1 TBS coconut aminos OR organic
tamari soy sauce

Makes 6 servings

Directions:

1 Add the chicken, curry, onion, garlic, coconut milk, red peppers, tomato sauce, natural sweetener in a 4-quart slow cooker on low. Add salt, pepper and coconut oil. Cover and cook for 6-8 hours or until chicken is fork tender. Shred with a fork and serve over curry "rice."

2 To make the rice, place the cauliflower in a food processor and process into "rice." Heat oil in a medium saucepan over low heat. Sauté the garlic; when the garlic becomes aromatic, slowly stir in cumin, curry powder and chili powder. When spices begin to fry and become fragrant, stir in the broth and a little water. Increase heat to high and add the soy sauce. Just before the mixture comes to a boil, stir in cauliflower rice. Bring to a rolling boil; reduce heat to low, cover, and simmer 15 to 20 minutes, or until all liquid is absorbed. Remove from heat and let stand 5 minutes.

Nutritional Comparison (per serving):

Item	Calories	Fat	Protein	Carbs	Fiber	Effective Carbs
Traditional Chicken Curry	609	20g	49g	53.4g	2g	51.4g
"Healthified" Chicken Curry	400	20g	47g	7.7g	3.1g	4.6g

Chicken Tikka Masala

Ingredients:

½ c. onion, chopped

1 jalapeño, chopped

1-inch piece fresh ginger, peeled and minced

4 boneless chicken breasts, cubed into ½ inch pieces

½ c. tikka masala curry paste

1 (14-oz.) can diced tomatoes

1 (14-oz.) can coconut milk

¼ c. fresh cilantro leaves, chopped

½ tsp Celtic sea salt

½ tsp black pepper

Directions:

1 Place all ingredients in a 4-quart slow cooker and set on low for 6-8 hours. Stir well before serving. Serve over cauliflower "rice" (see page 17) or Miracle rice.

Nutritional Comparison (per serving):

Item	Calories	Fat	Protein	Carbs	Fiber	Effective Carbs
Traditional Chicken Tikka Masala	535	24.6g	30g	45.6g	4.6g	41g
"Healthified" Chicken Tikka Masala	366	24.2g	29.5g	8g	2.6g	5.4g

Makes 6 servings

Butter Chicken

Ingredients:

4 boneless chicken thighs and drumsticks

½ c. onion, halved and thinly sliced

1 TBS ginger, grated

4 cloves garlic, crushed

1 TBS chili powder

2 tsp curry powder

¼ tsp cinnamon

2 c. diced tomatoes

2 TBS tomato paste

1-2 tsp garam masala

1 ½ c. cottage cheese

Celtic sea salt and pepper to taste

cauliflower rice or Miracle rice

Directions:

1　Place everything but the cottage cheese, salt and pepper in a 4-quart slow cooker.

2　Cover and cook on low for 6-8 hours.

3　Uncover, stir in the cottage cheese, season to taste with salt and pepper. Heat until cottage cheese is melted and serve over cauliflower "rice" (see page 17) or Miracle rice.

Nutritional Comparison (per serving):

Item	Calories	Fat	Protein	Carbs	Fiber	Effective Carbs
Traditional Butter Chicken	385	5.7g	32g	48.4g	3.1g	45.3g
"Healthified" Butter Chicken	214	5..3g	30.6g	10g	3g	7g

Makes 4 servings

Chicken Makhani

Ingredients:

15 cardamom pods
    (sewn together)

2 lbs boneless skinless chicken
    thighs (frozen works fine)

½ c. onion, sliced

6 garlic cloves, chopped

2 tsp curry or 2 TBS curry
    leaves, chopped

½ tsp cayenne pepper

2 tsp garam masala

½ tsp ground ginger

4 TBS butter or coconut oil

1 c. tomato sauce

2 TBS lemon juice

1 can coconut milk

1 c. coconut kefir OR plain
    Greek yogurt

Celtic sea salt to taste

4 packages Miracle Rice

Makes 8 servings

Directions:

1   Sew together the cardamom pods using a needle and thread or bundle in a cheese cloth (so you can remove them at the end).

2   Place the chicken in a 5-quart slow cooker, and add onion, garlic, and all of the dry spices. Add the butter, tomato sauce, lemon juice and coconut milk.

3   Cover and cook on low for 6 to 8 hours.

4   The chicken will shred easily with 2 forks when fully cooked. Stir in coconut kefir or plain yogurt 15 minutes before serving. Discard cardamom pods. Salt to taste, serve over Miracle Rice and with "Healthified" Naan Bread (see page 164).

NAAN Bread is an oven-baked flatbread. It is one of the most popular varieties of South Asian breads and is particularly popular in India. It works great for picking up food instead of using utensils. It makes for a fun dinner...unless you are in charge of clean up! (see page 164.)

Nutritional Comparison (per serving):

Item	Calories	Fat	Protein	Carbs	Fiber	Effective Carbs
Traditional Makhani	527	28g	37g	55.1g	2.4g	52.7g
"Healthified" Makhani	420	28g	35g	7g	2.2g	4.8g

Indian Chicken and Cauliflower

Ingredients:

4 (8-oz.) chicken breasts

1 c. onion, chunks

1 4-inch piece fresh ginger

2 c. tomatoes, diced

1 clove garlic

1 TBS Celtic sea salt

1 TBS turmeric

1 TBS garam masala

1 TBS red chili powder

¼ c. coconut oil, melted

1 c. coconut milk

3 Serrano peppers or 6 jalapeño peppers

1 cinnamon stick

4 green cardamom pods

6 cloves

1 large head of cauliflower

Makes 8 servings

Directions:

1 Place the chicken in a 4-quart slow cooker (frozen is fine, but will need an extra 45 minutes of cooking time).

2 Peel onion and ginger and cut in 1-inch pieces. Place onion, ginger and tomatoes in a food processor and grind until a smooth paste. Add garlic. salt, turmeric, garam masala, red chili powder, oil, and coconut milk. Run processor to mix with paste and then pour over chicken. Split chilies in half and remove stems. Add cinnamon stick, cardamom pods, cloves, and green chilies to slow cooker and stir well to combine.

3 Cover and cook on low for 5 hours.

4 Cut the cauliflower into flowerettes and add the flowerettes to the slow cooker, mixing the cauliflower into the mixture. Cover and cook another 3 hours. Using 2 forks, shred the chicken. Remove cinnamon stick and cardamom pods and enjoy!

Nutritional Comparison (per serving):

Item	Calories	Fat	Protein	Carbs	Fiber	Effective Carbs
Traditional Indian Chicken	490	25g	21g	46.3g	4g	42.3g
"Healthified" Indian Chicken	321	24g	18g	9g	3.5g	5.5g

Curry Chicken

Ingredients:

6 bone-in chicken thighs

6 cloves garlic, minced

2-inch piece fresh ginger, minced

4 TBS curry powder

3 c. organic chicken broth

2 c. Coconut Milk Kefir or plain
Greek yogurt

1 ½ TBS Celtic sea salt

Freshly ground black pepper

1 red pepper, cut in slices

1 yellow pepper, cut in slices

1 green pepper, cut in slices

1 lemon, cut in wedges

cauliflower rice (see page 17) or
Miracle rice

Directions:

1 Place all the ingredients except the lemon wedge and "rice" in a 4-quart slow cooker. Cover and cook on low for 6 to 8 hours. The chicken will fall off the bone when it is ready to serve.

2 Divide curry evenly into bowls. Serve with a wedge of lemon. Serve over cauliflower "rice" and with NAAN Bread (see page 164.)

This dish is real comfort food! In the curry recipe, I substituted Coconut Milk Kefir in place of 1 cup yogurt and ¾ cup coconut milk. I save a TON of calories, carbs and fat (for those of you who count fat grams:). Kefir is a cultured, enzyme-rich food filled with friendly micro-organisms that helps balance your "inner ecosystem." More nutritious and therapeutic than yogurt, it supplies complete protein, essential minerals, and valuable B vitamins. Just make sure to purchase the "original" version...the vanilla has a ton of unwanted sugar.

Nutritional Comparison (per serving):

Item	Calories	Fat	Protein	Carbs	Fiber	Effective Carbs
Traditional Curry	448	12g	50g	33g	3g	30g
"Healthified" Curry	366	12g	48g	6.2g	3g	3.2g

Makes 6 servings

Coconut Kefir

Are you looking for a thick, tasty beverage? or something to add to your protein smoothie? Try this. It has less calories than skim milk, and only 3 grams of sugar (versus 12 for skim milk...skim milk is high in lactose; but after childhood we slowly lose the enzyme to break this down..."lactose intolerance"). Coconut Kefir also has 10 live and active cultures for good bacteria. Feeding your body delicious fermented foods and drinks is a great way to boost your brain-body connection. Did you know that the health of your intestines affects your moods, behavior and brain health?

Our moods are directly correlated to the intestinal flora of our gut...the nervous system actually comes from the gut to the brain (in the past they thought it was the other way). Check out the nutritional analysis compared to regular yogurt! WOW!

Item	Calories	Carbs	Sugar	Fiber
Yoplait Yogurt	175	35g	28g	0g
Plain Yogurt	120	17g	10g	1g
Coconut Milk KEFIR	70	6g	3g	3g

NAAN Bread

Ingredients:

3 egg whites

½ tsp cream of tartar

3 oz. Sour Cream or coconut cream

½ c. Jay Robb unflavored whey
    or egg white protein

OPTIONAL:

1 tsp curry powder

Directions:

1   Whip the whites in a clean, dry, cool bowl for a few minutes until VERY stiff. Blend in the whey protein and sour cream (or softened coconut cream). Heat the oil in a fry pan on medium high until a drop of water will sizzle. Once it is hot, place a circle of dough on the pan. Fry until golden brown on both sides. Remove from heat and place on a plate. Enjoy!

Nutritional Comparison (per serving):

Item	Calories	Fat	Protein	Carbs	Fiber	Effective Carbs
Traditional NAAN Bread	155	4.5g	6g	22g	1g	21g
"Healthified" NAAN Bread	73	4.5	6.6g	1.5g	0g	1.5g

Makes 4 servings

Coconut Chicken and NAAN

Ingredients:

2 skinless, boneless chicken
    breast, cut in bite-size pieces

1 ¾ c. coconut milk kefir

1 TBS tomato paste

½ small onion, chopped

2 cloves garlic, minced

3 TBS curry powder

1 tsp cinnamon

1 tsp paprika

1 bay leaf

½ tsp grated fresh ginger root

2 tsp Swerve, Confectioners
    (or equivalent)

Celtic sea salt to taste

½ lemon, juiced

½ tsp cayenne pepper

Directions:

1 Place the chicken, coconut kefir, tomato paste, onion, garlic, curry powder, cinnamon, paprika, bay leaf, ginger, natural sweetener and salt in a 4-quart slow cooker.

2 Cover and cook for 6-8 hours or until the chicken is fully cooked and flavors have melded. Remove bay leaf, and stir in lemon juice and cayenne pepper.

Nutritional Comparison (per serving):

Item	Calories	Fat	Protein	Carbs	Fiber	Effective Carbs
Traditional Chicken Curry	313	21.7g	13g	14g	3.7g	10.3g
"Healthified" Chicken Curry	122	4.6g	13g	8.3g	3.7g	4.6g

Makes 4 servings

Mexican Lasagna

Ingredients:

1 lb grass fed ground hamburger

½ c. chopped onion

1 (7-oz.) can green chile peppers

2 TBS of taco seasoning (see below)

½ c. tomato sauce or salsa

2 eggs

2 c. cottage cheese

1 tsp Celtic sea salt

¼ tsp freshly ground black pepper

1 lb thinly sliced turkey
　　(for "noodle layer)

2 c. shredded Monterrey Jack cheese

1 (10-oz.) can tomato sauce or salsa

TACO SEASONING:

2 TBS Chili Powder

½ tsp Garlic Powder

½ tsp Onion Powder

½ tsp crushed Red Pepper Flakes

½ tsp dried Oregano

1 tsp Paprika

3 tsp ground Cumin

2 tsp Celtic Sea Salt

2 tsp fresh ground black pepper

Makes 6 servings (Lasagna)
Makes 20 servings (seasoning)

Directions:

1　To make the meat mixture, heat oil in medium skillet over medium high heat. Add ground beef, onion, green chile peppers and sauté until browned. Add taco seasoning and ½ cup tomato sauce and let simmer on low for 3 minutes.

2　Meanwhile, make the cheese mixture. In a medium bowl mix eggs with cottage cheese and season with salt and pepper; stir until well blended.

3　To assemble the casserole, layer the bottom of a 4-quart slow cooker with ½ the tomato sauce, top that with the meat mixture. Place a layer of "healthified" protein noodles (the thinly sliced turkey), then top that with ½ the cottage cheese mixture. Place a layer of Monterey Jack cheese on top of the cottage cheese. Repeat the layering one more time. Top with tomato sauce and remaining shredded cheese.

4　Cook on low for 4-5 hours or until the cheese is melted.

TACO SEASONING DIRECTIONS: In a bowl, mix together all ingredients. Store in an airtight container.

Nutritional Comparison (per serving):

Item	Calories	Fat	Protein	Carbs	Fiber	Effective Carbs
Traditional Lasagna	548	31g	33g	34.4g	4g	30.4g
"Healthified" Lasagna	417	30g	43g	5g	3g	2g
Store Bought Taco Seasoning	15	0g	0g	4g	0g	4g
"Healthified" Taco Seasoning	5	0.2g	0.2g	0.9g	0.4g	0.5g

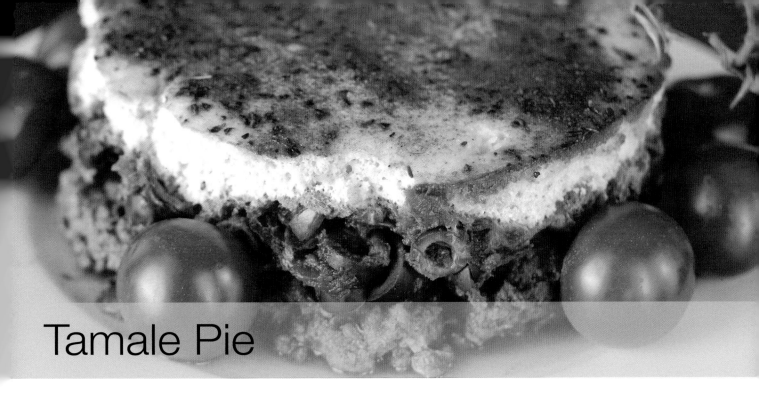

Tamale Pie

Ingredients:

1 lb grass fed ground beef

½ c. chopped onion

1 large green bell pepper, chopped

3 c. salsa

1 (4-oz.) can sliced ripe olives

2 cloves garlic, minced

½ tsp Celtic sea salt

2 tsp chili powder

½ tsp black pepper

CRUST:

½ c. coconut flour

8 eggs

½ tsp Celtic sea salt

½ tsp chili powder

1 c. white cheddar, freshly shredded

2 tsp Taco spices (page 166)

Directions:

1 In a skillet, brown the ground beef with onions and green pepper; drain well. Add salsa, olives, garlic, salt, chili powder and black pepper. Reduce heat and simmer, uncovered, for about 20 minutes, or until thickened. Set filling aside.

2 In a food processor or large bowl, combine coconut flour, eggs, salt, chili powder, and cheese. Blend until smooth.

3 Spread the meat mixture in a greased 4-quart slow cooker. Spread the corn bread mixture over the top, sprinkle with Taco spices, cover and cook on low for 5-6 hours or until cornbread is cooked through.

Nutritional Comparison (per serving):

Item	Calories	Fat	Protein	Carbs	Fiber	Effective Carbs
Traditional Tamale Pie	430	19g	23g	25g	3g	22g
"Healthified" Tamale Pie	313	17g	23g	13g	6g	7g

Makes 8 servings

Fajitas

Ingredients:

½ c. onion, sliced

3 sweet peppers, sliced

1 ½ lbs grass fed beef roast or
    boneless chicken breast

½ c. organic beef or chicken broth

½ tsp Celtic sea salt

2 TBS cumin

1 ½ TBS chili powder

Squirt of lime juice

"Healthified" Tortillas

Fajita fixings

"HEALTHIFIED" TORTILLAS:

1 1/4 c. blanched almond flour
    (or 1/2 c. coconut flour)

5 TBS psyllium husk powder

1 tsp Celtic sea salt

2 TBS butter

2 eggs (4 if using coconut flour)

1 c. hot water

Makes 12 servings

Directions:

1   Place the sliced onion and peppers in the bottom of a 4-quart slow cooker. Lay beef or chicken on top of veggies. Pour beef or chicken broth over top. Sprinkle everything with cumin, salt, and chili powder. Squirt lime juice over the top. Cover and cook on low for 7 to 8 hours.

2   When meat is done, shred with two forks and stir back in with juices. Serve meat mixture with slotted spoon on "healthified" tortillas (or lettuce leaves for Pure Protein and Fat days) and with your choice of fixings.

TORTILLAS:

In a medium sized bowl, combine the almond/coconut flour, psyllium powder (no substitutes: flaxseed meal won't work), and salt. Add in the eggs and combine until a thick dough. Boil the water (or marinara) and add into the bowl. Mix until well combined. Let sit for a minute or two until the dough gels up. Separate into 10 balls (about 2 inches in diameter). Place the dough onto a piece of greased parchment paper. Top with another greased piece of parchment. Using a rolling pin, roll the dough out in a circle shape with even thickness throughout. This dough is very forgiving, so if you don't make a circle with the rolling pin, use your hands to perfect your tortilla. Heat a large pan to medium-high heat with coconut oil or coconut oil spray. Once hot, place an unbaked tortilla on the pan (if the tortilla sticks to the parchment the first time, as it did for me, use your hands to close up any holes...the dough is still very forgiving) and sauté until light brown, then flip and bake through.

Nutritional Comparison (per serving):

Item	Calories	Fat	Protein	Carbs	Fiber	Effective Carbs
Traditional Fajitas	240	6.7g	28g	16g	3g	13g
"Healthified" Fajitas	187	6.1g	29g	5.8g	3g	2.5g

Picadillo

Ingredients:

1 TBS coconut oil

2 lbs ground bison or grass fed
　　ground beef

4 oz. chorizo-style cooked
　　chicken sausage, diced

1 TBS chili powder

2 tsp cumin

1 tsp oregano

½ tsp cinnamon

½ c. organic beef broth

2 TBS tomato paste

2 TBS red-wine vinegar

½ c. diced onion

2 c. chipotle or Anaheim
　　peppers, chopped and seeded

½ c. pitted green olives, sliced

5 cloves garlic, minced

2 c. diced tomatoes

¼ tsp Celtic sea salt

¼ tsp freshly ground pepper

Garnish with slivered almond

Makes 8 servings

Directions:

1　Heat oil in a large skillet over medium heat. Add bison (or beef) and cook, breaking up the meat with a spoon, for 5 to 6 minutes. If necessary, transfer to a colander and drain any extra fat, then return to the skillet. Add sausage, chili powder, cumin, oregano and cinnamon; cook over medium-high heat, stirring for about 1 to 2 minutes. Add in broth, tomato paste and vinegar until combined.

2　Transfer the meat mixture to a 5-quart slow cooker. Stir in onion, peppers, olives and garlic. Add tomatoes with their juice. Cover and cook on low for 6-8 hours. Stir the picadillo to combine and season with salt and pepper. Garnish with slivered almonds if desired.

Nutritional Comparison (per serving):

Item	Calories	Fat	Protein	Carbs	Fiber	Effective Carbs
Traditional Picadillo	498	20.9	32g	41.9g	2g	39.9g
"Healthified" Picadillo	329	20g	30.6g	4.8g	1.5g	3.3g

Creamy Mexican Chicken

Ingredients:

2 lbs uncooked frozen chicken breast

1½ c. diced tomatoes

16 oz. salsa

8 oz. cream cheese

Directions:

1 Place the frozen chicken breasts in a 4-quart slow cooker, top with tomatoes and salsa. Cook on low for 6 to 8 hours or until chicken is cooked.

2 Place block of cream cheese on top. Cook for an additional 30 minutes. Whisk to incorporate cream cheese into sauce. The stirring will cause the chicken to shred.

3 Serve on top of cauliflower rice (see page 17) or Miracle rice. Serve with extra salsa if desired.

NOTE: This has been a favorite recipe of my clients and their families.

Nutritional Comparison (per serving):

Item	Calories	Fat	Protein	Carbs	Fiber	Effective Carbs
Traditional Dish with White Rice	490	17.6g	40g	42g	3.3g	38.7g
"Healthified" Chicken	349	17.4g	37.3g	8g	2.8g	5.2g

Makes 6 servings

Chicken Mole

Ingredients:

4 lbs boneless, skinless chicken thighs or legs

1 tsp Celtic sea salt

2 c. diced tomatoes

½ c. onion, finely chopped

2 dried ancho chiles, stemmed

1 large chipotle chile

½ c. sliced almonds, toasted

3 oz. unsweetened chocolate, finely chopped (½ c.)

¼ c. Swerve, Confectioners (or equivalent) NOTE: Nature's Hollow Xylitol Honey works great too

3 garlic cloves, smashed and peeled

3 TBS coconut oil or butter

¾ tsp ground cumin

½ tsp ground cinnamon

Makes 12 servings

Directions:

1 Season chicken thighs with salt and place in a 5-quart slow cooker. In a blender, puree tomatoes, onion, ancho and chipotle chiles, almonds, chocolate, natural sweetener, garlic, oil, cumin, and cinnamon until smooth. Add tomato mixture to slow cooker, cover, and cook on high until chicken is tender, 4 hours (or 8 hours on low). Serve chicken with sauce over cauliflower "rice" (see page 17) or Miracle rice.

Nutritional Comparison (per serving):

Item	Calories	Fat	Protein	Carbs	Fiber	Effective Carbs
Traditional Chicken Mole	543	20.6g	48g	45g	2.5g	42.5g
"Healthified" Chicken Mole	384	20g	45.8g	4.8g	2.1g	2.7g

Doro Watt

Ingredients:

2 large onions, chopped fine

1 clove garlic, minced

½ c. butter or coconut oil

4 TBS Organic Ethiopian Berebere (spice)

1 tsp Celtic sea salt

1 whole chicken, separate legs, breasts, thighs

8 organic hard boiled eggs

Directions:

1 Chop the onions and place in a slow cooker with the garlic and butter/oil, Berebere and salt. Turn on low and let sit over night or until the onions caramelize (at least 8 hours).

2 In the morning (or after 8 hours), place the chicken in the slow cooker and let it cook for another 8 hours (the chicken will fall off the bone when it is ready to serve).

3 Meanwhile, cook the hard boiled eggs. Place the chicken/onion mixture in a beautiful dish and mix in the hard boiled eggs.

ETHIOPIA:

This is a very special dish to my family! When we were in Ethiopia, one of the things we ate all the time was Doro Watt. It is a traditional dish that is made with lots of onions, chicken and hard boiled eggs. The trick is the spice they use. Craig found a mixture of the spice called Berebere (that way I didn't have to buy a million spices for this dish). We just ordered another canister because, as you can see, the boys LOVE this dish! I asked Micah if he remembers eating it in Ethiopia but he didn't really answer... I think he was in food heaven! As you can see, they could hardly wait for me to finishing taking the photos!

Nutritional Comparison (per serving):

Item	Calories	Fat	Protein	Carbs	Fiber	Effective Carbs
"Healthified" Doro Watt	338	22.7g	39g	3.8g	0.6g	3.2g

Makes 8 servings

Moroccan Beef

Ingredients:

½ c. sliced onion

2 lb grass fed beef roast

2-4 TBS organic garam masala

1 tsp Celtic sea salt

Directions:

1 Slice the onion in thin strips. Place in a 4-quart slow cooker. Place the beef roast in the slow cooker on top of the onions. Add the spices and salt. Cook on low for 8 hours.

2 Shred the beef with a fork and cook on keep-warm setting for another 2 hours for the spices to infuse the beef. Serve over Miracle Rice, cauliflower "rice" (see page 17) or in a "Healthified" tortilla (see page 168)!

Nutritional Comparison (per serving):

Item	Calories	Fat	Protein	Carbs	Fiber	Effective Carbs
Traditional Beef With Rice	378	9.8g	32g	38g	0.7g	37.3g
"Healthified" Beef	209	9.5g	30.4g	0.7g	0g	0.7g

Makes 8 servings

Shrimp Etouffée

Ingredients:

3 TBS coconut oil

1 yellow onion, peeled and chopped

3 strips bacon, chopped

1/4 tsp Celtic sea salt

1/2 green bell pepper, chopped

3 cloves garlic, peeled and crushed

3 TBS tomato paste

2 bay leaves

1 TBS whole basil leaves

1 TBS whole thyme leaves

1/4 tsp freshly ground black pepper

4 green onions, chopped

1 1/2 pounds shrimp, peeled

cauliflower "rice" (see page 17)

Makes 8 servings

Directions:

1 In a 4 quart or larger slow cooker add the oil, onions, bacon pieces and salt. Turn slow cooker on high and caramelize the onions until golden and very soft, for about 1-2 hours.

2 Turn slow cooker to low-medium and add the remaining ingredients, except the shrimp and rice. Cover and cook for 2-6 hours (the longer, the more the flavors will open up).

3 Add the shrimp and cook for 30 minutes or until the shrimp are cooked through and are no longer translucent. Place the mixture onto a beautiful serving dish and garnish with green onions. Serve over "cauliflower" rice.

Nutritional Comparison (per serving):

Item	Calories	Fat	Protein	Carbs	Fiber	Effective Carbs
Traditional Etouffée	222	7g	25g	15g	3g	12g
"Healthified" Etouffée	201	5.8g	22.7g	5.2g	0.9g	4.3g

Glazed Pumpkin Bread

Ingredients:

3 c. blanched almond flour

½ tsp Celtic sea salt

1 tsp baking soda

2 tsp ground cinnamon

1 tsp ground nutmeg

1 tsp ground ginger

¼ tsp ground cloves

¼ c. butter or Coconut Oil

1 c. Swerve, Confectioners
(or equivalent)

6 large eggs

2 c. fresh OR canned pumpkin

GLAZE:

1 c. coconut oil, melted

½ c. Swerve, Confectioners
(or equivalent)

Directions:

1 In a mixing bowl combine almond flour, baking soda, salt, and spices. Mix butter, natural sweetener, eggs and pumpkin until smooth. Stir wet ingredients into dry. Pour in a greased 2-quart mold (whatever you use, make sure it fits in your slow cooker). Place in slow cooker. Cover and bake on high for 3 to 4 hours.

2 To make the glaze, mix ingredients together in a small bowl and spoon over warm bread. Allow to cool before cutting and serving.

Nutritional Comparison (per serving):

Item	Calories	Fat	Protein	Carbs	Fiber	Effective Carbs
Traditional Pumpkin Bread	230	14g	2g	40g	1.9g	38.1g
"Healthified" Pumpkin Bread	191	14g	7.3g	7.5g	3.5g	4.2g

Makes 16 servings

Zucchini Bread

Ingredients:

1 c. shredded zucchini

10 eggs (or 6 eggs and 1 c.
    coconut milk)

¾ c. butter or coconut oil, melted

¼ c. Swerve, Granular
    (or equivalent)

2 tsp cinnamon

1 tsp nutmeg

½ tsp ginger

1 tsp Celtic sea salt

1 c. coconut flour

1 tsp aluminum free baking powder

1 tsp vanilla extract

GLAZE:

1 c. coconut oil

1 c. Swerve, Confectioners
    (or equivalent)

Directions:

1   In mixing bowl with hand-held electric mixer, beat eggs until light and foamy. Add oil, natural sweetener, grated zucchini and vanilla. Mix well. Stir dry ingredients with nuts; stir in zucchini mixture and blend well.

2   Pour in a greased 2-quart mold (whatever you use, make sure it fits in your slow cooker). Place in slow cooker. Cover and bake on high for 3 to 4 hours. Do not remove cover to check cake until it has cooked for 3 hours.

3   Let stand 5 minutes before removing from the mold. Drizzle with glaze. Allow to cool before cutting and serving.

Nutritional Comparison (per serving):

Item	Calories	Fat	Protein	Carbs	Fiber	Effective Carbs
Traditional Zucchini Bread	379	25g	4.1g	40.1g	1.1g	39g
"Healthified" Zucchini Bread	268	25g	4.8g	4.8g	2.8g	2g

Makes 16 servings

Fudge

Ingredients:

8 oz. unsweetened chocolate squares, chopped

1 ½ c. natural peanut butter or almond butter

1 ¾ c. unsweetened almond milk

2 ½ c. Swerve, Confectioners (or equivalent to taste)

½ tsp vanilla

¼ tsp Celtic sea salt

Directions:

1 Place the chocolate, peanut or sunflower butter, almond milk and natural sweetener in a 2-quart slow cooker.

2 Cover and cook on low 30 minutes, stir well, then cover and cook for 2 hours without lifting the lid.

3 After 2 hours, turn the slow cooker off, uncover, add vanilla and stir to combine ingredients. Allow to cool in uncovered slow cooker, until fudge has reached room temperature (about 30 to 60 minutes).

4 Using a large spoon or hand mixer, stir vigorously for 5 minutes or until it loses some of the gloss. Lightly grease a 1-quart casserole dish. Pour fudge in a dish, cover and refrigerate 4 hours or until firm. Cut into 30 pieces.

Fudge is perfect for the slow cooker because it doesn't scorch or burn.

Nutritional Comparison (per serving):

Item	Calories	Fat	Protein	Carbs	Fiber	Effective Carbs
Traditional Fudge	207	12.9g	5g	21.6g	2g	19.6g
"Healthified" Fudge	120	10.5g	5g	4.7g	2.1g	2.6g

Makes 30 servings

Crème Brûlée

Ingredients:

5 egg yolks

2 c. heavy cream

½ c. Swerve, Confectioners
　　(or equivalent)

1 TBS pure vanilla

¼ c. Swerve, Granular or xylitol
　　(for topping)

Directions:

1　Insert a heat-resistant dish that fits inside of your slow cooker insert. Using a pitcher, pour water around the edges so there is water ½ - ¾ of the way up the sides of the dish. Take the dish back out. If you have separate dessert ramekins, do the same thing after placing them all inside.

2　To prepare the crème brûlée, whip the 5 egg yolks in a medium-sized bowl. Slowly add the cream, natural sweetener and vanilla. Mix well to combine. Pour the mixture in the dish and carefully lower into the stoneware without sloshing water into the dish. Cover and cook on high for 2-4 hours (1 to 2 hours for little ramekins). Custard should be set with the center still a bit jiggly. Touch lightly with your finger to check. Oven-baked crème brûlée is easy to over-bake, but in the slow cooker it is quite difficult.

3　Using gloves, carefully remove dish and let cool completely and chill in the refrigerator for 2-3 hours. Sprinkle the ¼ cup of natural sweetener evenly over the top of the custard. Move your oven rack to the top rung and broil for 3-10 minutes, checking often. The natural sweetener will broil and brown. Cool in the fridge for a few hours.

Nutritional Comparison (per serving):

Item	Calories	Fat	Protein	Carbs	Fiber	Effective Carbs
Traditional Crème Brûlée	419	27.8g	4.6g	40g	0g	40g
"Healthified" Crème Brûlée	274	27.8g	4.6g	2.4g	0g	2.4g

Makes 4 servings

Chocolate Torte

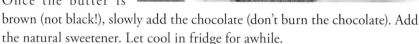

Ingredients:

14 TBS (1 ¾ sticks) butter or coconut oil

7 oz. unsweetened chocolate

1 ¼ c. Swerve, Confectioners (or equivalent) (adjust to desired sweetness)

5 large eggs

1 TBS coconut flour

Directions:

1 Brown the butter (if desired…tastes way better!) in a saucepan. Once the butter is brown (not black!), slowly add the chocolate (don't burn the chocolate). Add the natural sweetener. Let cool in fridge for awhile.

2 Once cool, add one egg at a time. Then add the coconut flour. Pour in a greased 2-quart mold (whatever you use, make sure it fits in your slow cooker). Place in slow cooker.

3 Cover and bake on high for 3 to 4 hours. Let cool before cutting.

Nutritional Comparison (per serving):

Item	Calories	Fat	Protein	Carbs	Fiber	Effective Carbs
Traditional Torte	333	24g	5g	27g	2.7g	24.3g
"Healthified" Torte	231	24g	5g	5.4g	3g	2.4g

Makes 12 servings

Chocolate Mousse

Ingredients:

2 c. heavy whipping cream

4 large egg yolks

1 ¼ c.Swerve, Confectioners (or equivalent) (adjust to desired sweetness)

⅓ c. espresso or strong coffee

1 tsp vanilla extract

1 c. unsweetened baking chocolate, chopped fine

Directions:

1 In a 4-quart slow cooker (if you use larger, it will cook faster), place the heavy cream, yolks, natural sweetener, espresso and extract. Whisk until combined. Add the chocolate.

2 Cover and cook on low for about two hours.

3 Once the chocolate is melted and there are little bubbles on top, carefully pour the mixture in a blender. Blend on high until it "grows" to almost double in size. Pour into serving dishes and chill for 2 hours or overnight in the refrigerator. Top with whipped cream if desired.

Nutritional Comparison (per serving):

Item	Calories	Fat	Protein	Carbs	Fiber	Effective Carbs
Traditional Mousse	336	22g	4.1g	37.4g	2.7g	34.1g
"Healthified" Mousse	214	22g	4.1g	6g	2.7g	3.3g

Makes 8 servings

Mocha Pudding Cake

Ingredients:

1 ⅓ c. Swerve, Confectioners (or equivalent) (adjust to desired sweetness)

1 c. blanched almond flour

½ c. coconut oil or unsalted butter, melted

4 large eggs, lightly beaten

⅓ c. unsweetened cocoa

¼ c. chopped pecans, toasted

1 shot espresso

½ tsp ground cinnamon

¼ tsp Celtic salt

2 tsp vanilla or butterscotch extract

Directions:

1 Stir together all ingredients in a large bowl. Line a 3-quart slow cooker with a greased piece of parchment paper or tinfoil (making sure the sides of the parchment go all the way up on the slow cooker so the mixture can't leak out. Pour the dough onto the parchment paper.

2 Cover and cook on low for 2 to 3 hours or until set around the edges but still soft in the center. Let stand, covered, 30 minutes.

3 Gently remove the parchment from the slow cooker and place onto a large serving dish (the cake can fall apart because it should be more of a pudding cake mix of melted goodness). Discard parchment paper and serve with a large spoon. Serve warm with "healthified" ice cream, if desired.

Nutritional Comparison (per serving):

Item	Calories	Fat	Protein	Carbs	Fiber	Effective Carbs
Traditional Pudding Cake	249	15g	3.8g	32g	1.3g	30.7g
"Healthified" Pudding Cake	179	17.1g	4.9g	3.7g	2g	1.7g

Makes 12 servings

Lemon Poppyseed Cake

Ingredients:

1 c. coconut oil or butter

1 c. Swerve, Granular
    (or equivalent)

4 eggs, room temperature

1½ tsp lemon extract

3 c. blanched almond flour

1 tsp baking powder

½ tsp Celtic sea salt

4 TBS poppyseeds

GLAZE:

2 TBS unsweetened almond milk

1 tsp lemon extract

1 c. Swerve, Confectioners
    (or equivalent)

Directions:

1   In a large bowl, use a mixer to cream butter and natural sweetener. Add eggs, one at a time, and lemon extract. In a separate bowl, sift almond flour, baking powder, and salt. Blend with creamed mixture. Fold in the poppyseeds. Cut waxed or parchment paper in an oval shape to fit 6-quart oval slow cooker; put in bottom of slow cooker. Pour batter on the parchment-lined slow cooker. Cover and cook on high for 3 hours, until toothpick inserted in the middle comes out clean.

2   When cool, place large oval plate on top of slow cooker insert. Flip over slow cooker so that the cake comes out onto the plate. Remove parchment paper (I trimmed the outside edges of my cake to make a loaf shape). Make glaze by whisking the almond milk, lemon extract and natural sweetener until smooth. Drizzle glaze over the top of the cake. Allow to cool before cutting and serving.

Nutritional Comparison (per serving):

Item	Calories	Fat	Protein	Carbs	Fiber	Effective Carbs
Traditional Cake	502	21g	3g	76g	1.5g	74.5g
"Healthified" Cake	226	23.2g	3.5g	3.6g	1.4g	2.2g

Makes 12 servings

Tropical Pudding Cake

Ingredients:

CAKE:

1 c. Swerve, Granular
   (or equivalent)

5 egg yolks

5 egg whites

⅓ c. unsweetened vanilla
   almond milk

1 tsp vanilla extract

1 c. blanched almond flour

1 ½ tsp baking powder

LECHES:

1 (14-oz.) can coconut milk

½ c. unsweetened vanilla
   almond milk

1 pint heavy whipping cream

1 TBS Swerve, Confectioners
   (or equivalent)

Directions:

1 In a large bowl, beat the egg yolks with ¾ cup sweetener until light in color and doubled in volume. Stir in almond milk, vanilla, almond flour, natural sweetener and baking powder. In another large bowl, beat egg whites until soft peaks form. Gradually add remaining ¼ cup sweetener. Beat until firm but not dry. Fold egg whites into yolk mixture. Pour in a greased 5-quart slow cooker and cook on medium for 4 hours.

2 Meanwhile make the leches topping by mixing together coconut milk, natural sweetener, almond milk and ¼ cup of the whipping cream in a medium sized bowl. Discard 1 cup of the measured milk mixture or cover and refrigerate. Pour remaining milk mixture over the finished cake slowly until absorbed. Whip the remaining whipping cream until it thickens and reaches spreading consistency. Frost cake with whipped cream.

Nutritional Comparison (per serving):

Item	Calories	Fat	Protein	Carbs	Fiber	Effective Carbs
Traditional Pudding Cake	499	28.5g	7.6g	54g	0g	54g
"Healthified" Pudding Cake	373	35g	8.3g	6.5g	1.6g	4.9g

Makes 8 servings

Bread Pudding

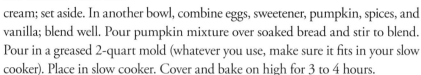

Ingredients:

1 loaf Pumpkin bread
(see page 174), cut in cubes

1 c. unsweetened almond milk
(or coconut milk)

½ c. heavy cream (or coconut milk)

3 large eggs

⅔ c. Swerve, Granular
(or equivalent)

2 c. pumpkin puree

1 tsp cinnamon

1 tsp pumpkin pie spice

1 tsp pure vanilla (or 1 vanilla bean)

½ tsp Celtic sea salt

Makes 18 servings

Directions:

1   In a large bowl, cover the cubed bread with the almond milk and cream; set aside. In another bowl, combine eggs, sweetener, pumpkin, spices, and vanilla; blend well. Pour pumpkin mixture over soaked bread and stir to blend. Pour in a greased 2-quart mold (whatever you use, make sure it fits in your slow cooker). Place in slow cooker. Cover and bake on high for 3 to 4 hours.

2   Serve with whipped cream, or "healthified" vanilla ice cream and "healthified" caramel sauce (recipes in "The Art of Healthy Eating - Sweets"). Makes 18 servings.

Nutritional Comparison (per serving):

Item	Calories	Fat	Protein	Carbs	Fiber	Effective Carbs
Traditional Bread Pudding	573	15.7g	5g	91g	3g	88g
"Healthified" Bread Pudding	204	15g	7.9g	9g	3.8g	5.2g

Tapioca Pudding

Ingredients:

2 c. unsweetened almond milk

1 c. canned coconut milk

⅔ c. Swerve, Confectioners
(or equivalent)

4 packages Miracle Rice, drained
and rinsed

4 eggs, lightly beaten

1 tsp vanilla (or other extract)

¼ tsp Celtic sea salt

Makes 8 servings

Directions:

1   Stir together the almond milk, coconut milk, natural sweetener, Miracle Rice, eggs, extract and salt in a slow cooker.

2   OPTION: Mix all the ingredients in a bowl, place the mixture in ramekins. Place the ramekins in the slow cooker. Slowly add water to the slow cooker, making sure to not get any water in the ramekins, and fill until the water is ⅔ up the ramekins.

3   Cover, and cook on Medium for 3 hours, or on Low for 6 hours, stirring occasionally. Serve warm.

NOTE: This is an acceptable dessert for a Pure Protein/Fat day! Yahoo!

Nutritional Comparison (per serving):

Item	Calories	Fat	Protein	Carbs	Fiber	Effective Carbs
Traditional Tapioca	191	5.2g	6g	31g	trace	31g
"Healthified" Tapioca	110	10g	3.7g	3.2g	1g	1.3g

Orange Cranberry Cake

Ingredients:

1 c. coconut oil or butter

2 c. Swerve, Granular
(or equivalent)

4 eggs, room temperature

1½ tsp orange extract

3 c. blanched almond flour

1 tsp baking powder

½ tsp Celtic sea salt

1 (6-oz.) pkg. fresh cranberries

GLAZE:

2 TBS unsweetened almond milk

1 tsp orange extract

1 c. Swerve, Confectioners
(or equivalent)

Directions:

1 In a large bowl, use a mixer to cream butter and natural sweetener. Add eggs, one at a time, and orange extract. In a separate bowl, sift almond flour, baking powder, and salt. Blend with creamed mixture. Fold in the cranberries. Cut waxed or parchment paper in an oval shape to fit 6-quart oval slow cooker; put in bottom of slow cooker. Pour batter in slow cooker. Cover and cook on high for 3 hours, until toothpick inserted in the middle comes out clean.

2 When cool, place large oval plate on top of slow cooker insert. Flip over slow cooker so that the cake comes out onto the plate. Remove waxed paper. Make glaze by whisking the almond milk, orange extract and natural sweetener until smooth. Drizzle glaze over the top of the cake.

Nutritional Comparison (per serving):

Item	Calories	Fat	Protein	Carbs	Fiber	Effective Carbs
Traditional Cake	502	21g	3g	76g	1.5g	74.5g
"Healthified" Cake	226	23.2g	3.5g	3.6g	1.4g	2.2g

Makes 12 servings

Cheesecake

Ingredients:

CRUST:

2 TBS butter or coconut oil

1 c. blanched almond flour

¼ c. Swerve, Granular
(or equivalent)

1 egg

FILLING:

12 oz. cream cheese, softened

½ c. Swerve, Confectioners
(or equivalent)

½ tsp vanilla

½ c. sour cream

3 eggs, lightly beaten

1 c. warm water

Directions:

1 Lightly coat a 1 ½-quart soufflé dish or casserole with coconut oil cooking spray. Tear off an 18x12-inch piece of heavy foil; cut in half lengthwise. Fold each piece lengthwise in thirds. Crisscross the foil strips and place the dish in the center of the crisscross (this helps to lift it out when it is done); set aside.

2 **CRUST:** Melt the butter/oil. Add in the almond flour, natural sweetener and egg. Press in dish. Set aside.

3 For filling, in a large bowl beat cream cheese, natural sweetener, and vanilla on medium speed until combined. Beat in sour cream until smooth. Add in eggs and mix on low speed just until combined. Pour filling in prepared dish. Cover dish tightly with foil. Pour warm water in a 3 ½- to 5-quart slow cooker. Using the ends of the foil strips, transfer dish to cooker. Leave foil strips under dish. Cover and cook on high-heat setting for 2 ½ hours or until center is set. Using foil strips carefully remove dish from cooker; discard foil strips. Cool completely, uncovered. Cover and chill for 4 to 24 hours before serving.

Nutritional Comparison (per serving):

Item	Calories	Fat	Protein	Carbs	Fiber	Effective Carbs
Traditional Cheesecake	244	17g	5.4g	22g	0g	22g
"Healthified" Cheesecake	214	19.6g	6.3g	3.3g	1g	2.3g

Makes 12 servings

Chocolate Raspberry Cheesecake

Ingredients:

CRUST:

2 TBS butter or coconut oil

1 ChocoPerfection bar (chocolate raspberry), chopped

1 c. almond flour (or hazelnut meal)

¼ c. Swerve, Granular (or equivalent)

1 tsp raspberry extract (if desired)

1 egg

FILLING:

2 oz. unsweetened baking chocolate, chopped

½ c. unsweetened almond milk

4 (8-oz.) packages cream cheese, room temperature

1 ½ c. Swerve, Confectioners (or equivalent)

¼ c. unsweetened cocoa powder

3 eggs

OPTIONAL:

1 c. raspberries

TOPPING:

¼ c. whipping cream

1 ChocoPerfection Bar (chocolate raspberry), chopped

2 TBS Swerve, Confectioners (or equivalent)

1 tsp raspberry extract (if desired)

Makes 16 servings

Directions:

1   Lightly coat a 1 ½-quart soufflé dish or casserole with coconut oil cooking spray. Tear off an 18x12-inch piece of heavy foil; cut in half lengthwise. Fold each piece lengthwise in thirds. Crisscross the foil strips and place the dish in the center of the crisscross (this helps to lift it out when it is done); set aside.

2   CRUST: Melt the butter/oil with the chopped ChocoPerfection bar. Stir until the chocolate is melted. Add in the nut meal, natural sweetener, egg and extract (if using). Press in the soufflé dish. Set aside.

3   FILLING: Stir chopped chocolate and almond milk in metal bowl set over saucepan of simmering water until melted and smooth. Remove bowl from over water. Blend cream cheese, natural sweetener, and cocoa powder in processor until smooth. Blend in eggs 1 at a time. Mix in lukewarm chocolate. Then swirl in the raspberries if desired. Pour filling over crust. Cover dish tightly with foil. Pour warm water in a 3 ½- to 5-quart slow cooker. Using the ends of the foil strips, transfer dish to cooker. Leave foil strips under dish. Cover and cook on high-heat setting for 2 ½ hours or until center is set. Using foil strips carefully remove dish from cooker; discard foil strips. Cool completely, uncovered, on a wire rack. Cover and chill for 4 to 24 hours before serving.

4   TOPPING: Stir cream and chocolate in a medium sized saucepan over low heat until smooth, add in the natural sweetener. Cool slightly. Pour over center of cheesecake, spreading to within ½ inch of edge and filling any cracks. Chill until topping is set, about 1 hour. Do ahead: Can be made 3 days ahead. Cover with foil and keep refrigerated.

Nutritional Comparison (per serving):

Item	Calories	Fat	Protein	Carbs	Fiber	Effective Carbs
Traditional Cheesecake	461	29.6g	7g	42.5g	1.9g	40.6g
"Healthified" Cheesecake	298	29g	7.7g	7.7g	4.3g	3.4g

Pumpkin Cheesecake

Ingredients:

CRUST:

1 c. pecans, crushed fine

3 TBS butter, melted

2 TBS Swerve, Granular
(or equivalent)

FILLING:

2 (8-oz.) packages cream cheese,
room temperature

1 ¼ c. Swerve, Confectioners
(or equivalent)

¾ c. sour cream

2 tsp vanilla

1 tsp cinnamon

½ tsp allspice

¼ tsp Celtic sea salt

4 eggs

1 (15-oz.) can pure pumpkin

SOUR CREAM TOPPING (OPTIONAL):

1 c. sour cream

3 TBS Swerve, Confectioners
(or equivalent)

1 tsp vanilla

Makes 12 servings

Directions:

1 Prepare a very large slow cooker (at least 6-quart) so a casserole dish can fit inside in a water bath. In a small bowl, combine melted butter with the crushed nuts and natural sweetener. Press the mixture in your casserole dish. Set aside.

2 In a large mixing bowl, combine the softened cream cheese, natural sweetener, sour cream, and vanilla extract. Add the spices and eggs. Mix well with a hand or stand mixer until smooth. Remove 1 cup of the cream cheese mixture and place in another bowl. Add the pumpkin to the 1 cup of cream cheese mixture. Pour half of the plain filling on top of the crust, swirl in ½ of the pumpkin mixture and repeat with remaining filling.

3 Put ½ to 1 cup of water in the bottom of your slow cooker. The inserted dish should push the water up to halfway up the sides of the cheesecake. Place the cheesecake in your slow cooker and cook on high for 2 to 4 hours or until the top is no longer jiggly. Unplug slow cooker and remove lid. In a small mixing bowl, whip together the sour cream topping. With a rubber spatula, very carefully spread the sour cream topping on top of the hot cheesecake. Let the cheese cake sit in the cooling slow cooker for an hour, before chilling in the refrigerator. Chill for at least 6 hours. Serve.

Nutritional Comparison (per serving):

Item	Calories	Fat	Protein	Carbs	Fiber	Effective Carbs
Traditional Cheesecake	192	7g	7.1g	27.5g	3.8g	23.7g
"Healthified" Cheesecake	128	7g	7.1g	10g	3.8g	6.2g

Pumpkin Pie Fondue

Ingredients:

2 c. pure pumpkin

4 oz. cream cheese

¼ c. unsweetened almond milk

½ c. Swerve, Confectioners (or equivalent)

1 tsp cinnamon

1 tsp Pumpkin Pie spice

Makes 8 servings

Directions:

1 Place all the ingredients in a food processor and puree until smooth. Place puree in a small dipper slow cooker.

2 Cover and cook on low for about an hour, stir well. Serve with "healthified" cookies (recipe in "Nutritious and Delicious" cookbook).

Nutritional Comparison (per serving):

Item	Calories	Fat	Protein	Carbs	Fiber	Effective Carbs
Traditional Pumpkin Fondue	125	5.7g	1.8g	18.8g	2g	16.8g
"Healthified" Pumpkin Fondue	73	5.3g	1.8g	5.8g	2g	3.8g

Pumpkin Custard

Ingredients:

3 c. pumpkin

6 eggs

¼ c. coconut milk, full fat

½ c. Swerve, Confectioners (or equivalent)

½ tsp ginger

½ tsp cinnamon

1 tsp vanilla extract

pinch of Celtic sea salt

Makes 6 servings

Directions:

1 Fill slow cooker with 1 inch water and turn on high. Allow to pre-heat for 30-45 minutes.

2 Place all the ingredients in a food processor or blender and puree until smooth. Pour in ramekins, filling almost to the top. Gently set in the water, stacking the ramekins if needed. Cover and cook on high for 4-6 hours.

3 Turn slow cooker off, and it will continue to stay warm for another hour or so, serve warm or cover and store in the fridge to serve chilled.

Nutritional Comparison (per serving):

Item	Calories	Fat	Protein	Carbs	Fiber	Effective Carbs
Traditional Custard	192	7g	7.1g	27.5g	3.8g	23.7g
"Healthified" Custard	128	7g	7.1g	10g	3.8g	6.2g

Pumpkin "Cup"cakes

Ingredients:

1 ½ c. blanched almond flour

¼ tsp Celtic sea salt

½ tsp baking soda

1 tsp ground cinnamon

½ tsp ground nutmeg

¼ tsp ground ginger

⅛ tsp ground cloves

2 TBS Butter or Coconut Oil

½ c. Swerve, Granular
(or equivalent)

3 large eggs

1 c. fresh OR canned pumpkin

FROSTING:

4 oz. cream cheese or coconut
cream

2 TBS unsweetened almond milk

3 TBS Swerve, Confectioners
(or equivalent)

Makes 12 servings

Directions:

1 Place a metal rack or trivet in a slow cooker. Grease cute tea cups. In a large bowl, combine all ingredients and beat until well blended. Spoon into teacups. Place the teacups in a 6-quart slow cooker. Gently put water in the slow cooker surrounding the teacups and filling the slow cooker to about ⅔ of the way up the teacups.

2 Cook on high for 3-4 hours or until the cupcakes are cooked all the way through and a toothpick comes out clean when you insert in the middle of the cupcake. Cool the cupcakes before frosting.

3 FROSTING. To make frosting, cream together cream cheese, almond milk and natural sweetener and place a dollop on top of each cupcake.

Nutritional Comparison (per serving):

Item	Calories	Fat	Protein	Carbs	Fiber	Effective Carbs
Traditional Pumpkin Cupcake	193	11g	4g	26g	1g	25g
"Healthified" Pumpkin Cupcake	160	13.2g	5.5g	5.2g	2.2g	3g

Chai Tea Cupcakes

Ingredients:

8 eggs

1 c. Swerve, Granular
(or equivalent)

2 TBS coconut oil or butter

4 chai tea bags steeped in
1 c. water

¾ c. coconut flour

1 tsp baking powder

1 tsp cinnamon

1 tsp vanilla

½ tsp Celtic sea salt

GLAZE:

1 c. coconut oil

1 c. Swerve, Confectioners
(or equivalent)

1 tsp cinnamon

Directions:

1. In a large bowl, combine the eggs, natural sweetener and oil. Steep 4 tea bags in 1 cup water for 5 minutes or until the water is saturated with chai goodness. Cool the tea for awhile, then slowly pour in the egg mixture (if you pour too fast and the water is too hot, it will cook the eggs).

2. In a separate bowl, combine the coconut flour, baking powder, cinnamon and salt. Mix the wet ingredients with the dry. Add the vanilla and stir until well combined.

3. Place the dough in cute greased tea cups. Place the tea cups in the largest slow cooker you own. Place water in the slow cooker to fill ⅔ of the way up the tea cups. (making sure not to get water in the cups).

4. Cover and cook on low for 2 to 4 hours.

5. To check if done, insert a clean toothpick in the center. If it comes out clean, it is baked through. Remove from slow cooker and let cool in for 10 minutes.

6. Meanwhile, melt coconut oil with natural sweetener and cinnamon. Drizzle baked cupcakes with the glaze. Enjoy!

Nutritional Comparison (per serving):

Item	Calories	Fat	Protein	Carbs	Fiber	Effective Carbs
Traditional Cupcake	311	15g	3g	43.4g	0.9g	42.3g
"Healthified" Cupcake	176	16.5g	3.6g	3.7g	2.2g	1.5g

Makes 16 servings

Cookie Dough Cupcakes

Ingredients:

CHOCOLATE CUPCAKES:

½ c. coconut flour

⅓ c. unsweetened cocoa powder

½ c. Swerve, Granular
(or equivalent)

½ tsp baking soda

½ tsp cinnamon

½ c. unsweetened almond milk

½ c. coconut oil or butter

5 eggs

1 tsp vanilla

COOKIE DOUGH FROSTING:

½ c. butter or coconut oil

½ c. Swerve, Confectioners
(or equivalent)

8 oz. cream cheese, softened
(or coconut cream if dairy allergy)

2 TBS unsweetened almond milk
(more to thin out frosting)

1 tsp vanilla extract

2 ChocoPerfection Bars,
chopped

Makes 12 servings

Directions:

1 In a large bowl, combine all the dry ingredients and blend well. Add the dry and wet ingredients and blend until smooth. Grease and fill cute teacups ⅔rds full. Place the teacups in a 6-quart slow cooker. Gently put water in the slow cooker surrounding the teacups and filling the slow cooker to about ⅔ of the way up the teacups. Cook on High for 3-4 hours or until the cupcakes are cooked all the way through and a toothpick comes out clean when you insert in the middle of the cupcake. Cool the cupcakes before frosting.

2 **TO MAKE THE FROSTING,** place the butter in a small saucepan and melt over medium-high heat (until it turns brown, not black). Add in natural sweeteners until dissolved and the mixture bubbles just a little. Using a hand mixer on low speed, add in cream cheese, almond milk and vanilla. Mix until combined. Once the mixture is totally cool (you don't want the chocolate to melt), stir in the chunks of ChocoPerfection. Use to frost cupcakes.

Nutritional Comparison (per serving):

Item	Calories	Fat	Protein	Carbs	Fiber	Effective Carbs
Traditional Cookie Dough Cupcake	391	26g	4g	35.1g	1.3g	33.8g
"Healthified" Cookie Dough Cupcake	267	26g	5g	4.8g	2.5g	2.3g

Chocolate Chip PB Cake

Ingredients:

½ c. coconut oil or butter

½ c. Swerve, Granular
(or equivalent)

½ c. Just Like brown sugar
(or equivalent)

3 eggs, beaten

½ c. natural peanut butter or
sunbutter

¾ c. sour cream

1 tsp vanilla extract

1 ¾ c. peanut or almond flour

1 tsp baking powder

½ tsp Celtic sea salt

2 ChocoPerfection Bars,
chopped

GLAZE:

2 TBS unsweetened almond milk

1 ½ TBS unsweetened cocoa
powder

½ c. Swerve, Confectioners
(or equivalent)

Makes 12 servings

Directions:

1 Cream butter and natural sweeteners (blending sweeteners = awesome flavor). Beat eggs in well. Mix in peanut butter, sour cream, and vanilla. In a separate bowl, combine peanut or almond flour, baking powder and salt together and add to creamed mixture. Stir in most of the ChocoPerfection chunks, reserving a few for the top. Spoon mixture in a greased 2 ½ to 3-quart soufflé dish or mold (which will fit in your slow cooker).

2 Place a small trivet (or fashion a little "ring" from aluminum foil) in the slow cooker, place the dish on the trivet, then cover the dish with 4 layers of paper towels. Cover loosely to allow steam to escape and cook on high for about 4 hours (test with a toothpick to check if done).

3 Meanwhile, mix the glaze ingredients in a small bowl. Cool in pot until dish is cool enough to handle, then transfer to a wire rack to cool completely. Once cool, cover in chocolate glaze.

Nutritional Comparison (per serving):

Item	Calories	Fat	Protein	Carbs	Fiber	Effective Carbs
Traditional Cake	405	22g	6g	46.6g	1.6g	45g
"Healthified" Cake	316	29g	11g	6.8g	2.7g	4.1g

Index